July 22nd, 2017

Blossom of the Golden Bell

Blossom of the Golden Bell

HWAIN CHANG LEE

Foreword by Dale T. Irvin

RESOURCE *Publications* · Eugene, Oregon

BLOSSOM OF THE GOLDEN BELL

Resource Publications
An Imprint of Wipf and Stock Publishers
199 W. 8th Ave., Suite 3
Eugene, OR 97401

www.wipfandstock.com

PAPERBACK ISBN: 978-1-5326-1138-4
HARDCOVER ISBN: 978-1-5326-1140-7
EBOOK ISBN: 978-1-5326-1139-1

Manufactured in the U.S.A.   OCTOBER 28, 2016

Contents

Endorsement

WHEN I RECEIVED THE manuscript of *Blossom of the Golden Bell*, six months had passed since I had sent my own manuscript about my memories of my mother's life to the publisher. Why was it that Hwain Chang Lee and I thought of our own mothers at almost the same time?

Though I have felt and appreciated the consideration shown to me by Hwain and her husband, I have never come to know her heart fully because we simply have not had the opportunity to share a deep conversation. As we have lived in such different environments, I wouldn't expect us to have much common ground. How did we both then come to this shared point of yearning after our mothers?

I believe that this common yearning connects us even across the distance of the Pacific Ocean. The same atmosphere I breathe she breathes as well on her side of the world. The same longing I feel she feels in turn in her own life.

We are living in the same increasingly alienating modern world. As our daily lives become more convenient and streamlined, as our knowledge and capacity grow, we are faced ever more with the hollowness of our lives and pursuits. The more accessible, convenient, and splendid the goods and gadgets we use, the more useless we ourselves begin to feel as machines replace human hands in nearly every workplace. A desolation of body and spirit, like that of an invalid prostrated on a hospital bed, makes us seek out our mothers.

Hwain's search and discovery of her mother through these written memories is the cry of our time, the cry of an infant seeking the milk of its mother's breast. It is a song of yearning for the warmth of a mother's embrace to fight the cold touch of our modern world.

How much can a person change? As Hwain reflects on her mother's life, she discovers how she herself has changed as a woman and how she continues to change as a human being, as she becomes a wife and mother of growing children in her own right. Her mother lived the life of a quintessential Korean matriarch even as the world around her was changing, even as she left her home country to live in a foreign land, experiencing all the while a confluence of joy, sorrow, love, and difficulty. This mother sought her own meaning and purpose in the Gospel of Christ, quietly striving to live by what she believed in a society rooted in Confucianism and virtuous obedience. She sought herself in this way not out of selfishness but in order to become the best mother to her children, to provide them with the best foundation of belief on which to live. She embraced the sorrow of loss, ultimately accepting her daughter Hwain no longer as a dependent but as a partner in the leadership of the family. She remained a faithful and dutiful wife to her ailing husband even as she gave her mind, heart, and purpose to her children, especially to her daughter Hwain.

Hwain's mother experienced the universal difficulties of the Korean matriarch, but she did not cede her life to the machinations fate. She was a strong, fighting woman who faced life's challenges with her own resourcefulness and purpose. However, she knew that her powers were limited and in her struggles she appealed to God, trusted him and sought him as a child seeks its mother's embrace. To live within this embrace was her ceaseless prayer, whether in times of joy or sorrow.

In Hwain's story I see so much that is universal. It is the story of motherhood, of Christian life, of a family of immigrants striving to succeed in a new land. Ultimately, however, I recognize in this collection of memories an author who has managed, in remembering her mother, to sublimate that life into something more. In writing of her mother's life she has found a vision of life and its meaning that is her own.

Dr. Byung Moo Ahan
Minjung Theologian, Professor
Han Guk Theological Seminary

Foreword

I HAVE HAD THE privilege of knowing and working with Dr. Hwain Chang Lee for nearly two decades now. I've long admired her engaging scholarship and her commitment to the work for justice and transformation in the wider community. I had gleaned from her bits and pieces of the story of her mother over the years, but nothing prepared me for the experience of reading *Blossom of the Golden Bell*. This is an extraordinary memoire, recounting more than the life of one woman or even one family as they journey from the village of Ha Myun Dae Bori first to Seoul and then to New York and New Jersey. *Blossom of the Golden Bell* tells the story of the struggles and triumph of an entire generation whose lives were part of the fabric of the so-called "The Miracle on the Han River." That story then crossed the Pacific to become an indelible part of the rich American experience.

Too many around the world know the story of Korea only through outside eyes. The horror of the Korean War is often little more than the backdrop for another M*A*S*H episode on American television where Koreans remain almost entirely absent, and when they do appear are marginal, subservient, or devious. The story of South Korea's post-war economic transformation is often little more than a textbook case study for export-oriented development in the 1960s. My own first encounter with aspects of the story that is told in *Blossom of the Golden Bell* was in the 1970s through various international organizations working for human rights in South Korea. Too often the actual lives of Koreans themselves, especially the women, got lost in these accountings. Little of the rich cultural and religious life and tradition made its way into the narratives others told. The disappointments, dreams, aspirations and agonies that were part of the fabric of the lives of Korean people that could be bound by enormously restrictive traditions and at the same time enormously hopeful were absent, if not silenced.

Blossom of the Golden Bell upends that narrative by telling the story of one woman and her extended family in a compelling and powerful manner. It shows in a moving way the manner in which her faith, courage, hope, determination, imagination, grace, mercy, and joy were combined, distilled, and passed along to her daughter and family. This is not just a historical memoire looking back across 75 years of recent history. By the end of the book it becomes an acute reminder of the blessings that those who have emigrated have brought to the United States. *Blossom of the Golden Bell* shows us that there are no outsiders, just human beings who live through tragedies and triumphs as they manifest their faith in God and demonstrate the resiliency of the human spirit.

Dale T. Irvin
President and Professor of World Christianity
New York Theological Seminary

Acknowledgments

MANY THANKS TO MY dear husband Bill for his love and support, and Dr. Marc Mullinax, Dr. Douglas Irvin and Joanne for their valuable guidance in putting this book together.

Prologue

The Mirror of the Bible

> Measure me by myself
>
> And not by time or love or space
>
> Or beauty.
>
> Give me this last grace:
>
> That I may be on my low stone
>
> A gage unto myself alone.
>
> I would not have these old faiths fall
>
> To prove that I was nothing at all.

—LAURA RIDING JACKSON

THE BIBLE TELLS MANY stories of women. In these women and in their world, we can see a reflection of ourselves and our own reality—physical, spiritual and social. Their stories, like mirrors, show us the conditions in which women lived during that time, and from which we can extract wisdom for today. In my mother's long life, the sorrows and triumphs of women like Mary and Martha echo and live on. Like these women, my mother possessed deep faith in her Lord.

Korean Christian women build their lives on two foundations. The first is the hard reality of the lives of women in the Bible. The second is the long history of Korean women born into a system of Confucian belief. What connects the two is *Han*, the Korean word meaning "the sorrow of a woman's suffering." My mother's story is a mingling and converging of these two realities.

These two traditions reflect our identities, as Korean women. Just as the souls of biblical women were transformed by their trying circumstances, so we are formed and changed in the gauntlet of suffering. Tears that no one sees are shed. Patience, never discerned, is endlessly tried. And from these trials, women emerge, formed with a new identity.

My mother gave me life, and gave her own life to me. She influenced me, taught me, and moved me. In return, I feel I must give her a gift. Since I cannot forget the stories of my mother's past, nor leave them unrecorded, my gift to my mother is this story I've written. I want these pages to reflect back to her, and to women like me, all the light she has given me.

This book is a friend—a stern but friendly mirror—that I offer to those mothers who suffer in silence because the weight of tradition is too great. I hope that readers will see the dialogue alive in their history, too, and in their own stories.

I.

Early Years

THE SECOND DAUGHTER

ON MARCH 1, 1919, thirty-three of Korea's political and religious leaders convened to sign a declaration of independence from 36 years of Japanese rule. My mother was born two weeks later, into a time of bloodshed. Her name was Yun Ae.

My mother was raised in a small rural town called Ha Myun Dae Bori in the Kapyung Koon region of Kyung-Ki-Do province. Her father worked as the chief manager in a Japanese company. Her family enjoyed a more comfortable style of life than the other villagers, and held a prominent place in the local hierarchy. She was the third of four children. Neither the eldest child nor a boy, my mother occupied a subordinate position in the Confucian family configuration. Her girlhood destined her to a life of service to those who were men, those who were weak, and those who were old. Her own needs and wants would have to come second.

My mother lived at home until she turned nine. In those days, free public education ended in the fourth grade, so she and her siblings were parceled out to the homes of different relatives in Seoul where they could attend schools in the capital city. My mother entered the Seoul Mi-Dong Elementary School as a 5th grader and later registered at the Bae-Hwa Girls' High School. She and her younger sister lived in the home of their father's younger brother. Each month, their father would send money for tuition, board, and rent.

As the eldest child and a boy, my mother's eldest brother had the right to the choicest accommodations. He had been welcomed into the home of his father's older sister, where his status in the familial hierarchy earned him his comfort. My mother's older sister experienced much of this same rightful comfort, and wanted for nothing. My mother and her younger sister were also treated according to their respective status in the family hierarchy. Though the household was never poor or short of food, the girls found their share was constantly scarce. A bowl of rice and a simple casserole would constitute their main meal of the day.

My mother's younger sister took full advantage of the rights the Confucian convention granted her. An older sister, as a woman, was expected to practice utter self-sacrifice. She was to devote herself to the fulfillment of her younger siblings' needs. More food! Better care! More attention! All of my mother's energy and rightful share she proffered to her younger sister.

During the summer and winter vacations, the scattered siblings reunited back home. Every summer their father, though largely absent himself, financed a vacation school that took place in a tent in the center of town where the local kids gathered to play sports and keep up their studies during the break. My mother and her four siblings served as the principal teachers, and this they greatly enjoyed. In the winter, their father provided a warm stove.

This was her father's pattern: he provided all the furnishings for the comfort and education of his children, but he was hardly ever present. He was a handsome, princely-looking man, a prominent figure in his community. At that time, such men could be on friendly terms with women other than their wives without turning any heads. When my mother was ten years old, while she and her

siblings were away at school, her father left home to be with another woman. From then on, he was married only in name.

§

My grandmother was a small woman, hardly any taller than four
feet, but of formidable force. She married one of the ancestors of
the Kyun clan, a descendant of a seventh-century king. The inher-
ent worthiness of royalty seemed to endure in her life. She im-
parted the pride of their heritage to her children, and taught them
to carry themselves with a sense of honor. She was a generous,
compassionate woman, and always bore herself with dignity.

Life would deal my grandmother many blows, as it did many
women like her. The path of her life diverged in innumerable ways
from where she had expected it to lead her. During her time, a
woman was accorded little right to expectation or even desire.
She had no means to achieve any life but that which her circumstances and other people obliged upon her. She had met her husband through a matchmaker, so she had not chosen the man she
married. Grandfather's infidelity was only one misfortune to be
borne. While the children were away he often drank heavily, and
would storm through the house in drunken rampages, tearing up
the rooms in search of things to harm. My grandmother turned to
faith to help her endure, but she knew she could no longer afford
to remain where he could reach her.

In that time, leaving one's husband, no matter the circumstances, was unthinkable. For a woman to put herself first, to
consider her own survival above her obligation to others, was to
lose her place in society and incur infamy. Few women chose this
course. I often wonder what drove my grandmother to make the
choice she did, what gave her the courage, and I think it must have
been her belief in what she deserved. A woman grew up learning,
then knowing, and finally believing that her life must revolve utterly around the life of a man. But my grandmother also had her
own faith. I believe that it was this faith in God that assured her
that she had worth, even if she was alone, apart from her man,
apart from her obligations. Her life had been mapped out for her,

but she found that there was more than one way to live. She had only to choose and, in doing so, to forge new paths into being.

Grandmother made the choice to leave her husband when my mother was in the eleventh grade, after 10 years of abuse. She fled to the home of a friend in the next town where she hid, working as a seamstress to earn her keep. After eight months, she left for Seoul, where she gathered her children just before their winter break. She told them that she had left their father, and they decided as a family to make themselves a new home in Seoul. They settled together in a modest apartment in the neighborhood of Kwang-hee Moon, near a Methodist Church. It was the winter my mother turned fifteen years old.

THE SEVENTEEN-YEAR-OLD TEACHER

August 3rd was the birthday of my mother's eldest sister. My aunt was in Japan at the time, studying after her graduation from Ewha University. To celebrate, mother and grandmother cooked mi-yuk gook, a seaweed soup cooked traditionally on birthdays. They sat eating somberly together at the table as steam from their bowls wafted up into their faces. It was two years since the family settled in Seoul, and mother's elder siblings had left to complete their studies and begin lives of their own in places of their own. Her youngest sister, too, had developed obligations and relationships outside of her family, and was rarely at home. My mother was 17 years old. The remaining women of the family continued their faithful church attendance at the Methodist Church, where my mother and her sister taught in the Sunday school. The family's only income was the wages grandmother earned as a seamstress and domestic worker.

They never saw grandfather, though he now lived in the next neighborhood with his mistress and their child—a five-year-old son. His proximity to the new life they'd created without him was a source of perpetual stress to grandmother. She had never quite clinched her escape. Grandfather remained ever close by, rendering the stability of their new life precarious. All that kept him from intruding was his own miraculous restraint, or perhaps his own lack of desire to reach them. Yet, the entirety of their lives still depended on what he might do if he chose to walk back in.

The two women were too solemn for the occasion. Their faces turned down over their soup so that the steam rose to dampen their cheeks. Mother and grandmother had lived alone for few years, and their intimacy made each sensitive to even the slightest rippling of feeling in the other. Each transmitted her apprehension to the other, and received it back again.

Their anxiousness never dissipated after they moved to Seoul. It kindled to a new intensity in their nerves. They lived, waiting. That afternoon grandmother and mother had gone to the local store to buy seaweed ("mi-yuk") for their little celebration. There they met, by a blow of chance—finally, it seemed, after all the time it'd waited to strike—grandfather's mistress. She had come to buy groceries for her family. They argued and made a scene. My mother erupted in anger, and warned the woman to leave her family alone, and they parted.

It was just after dark when they finished dinner. A loud knock sounded against the door. There was a pause. Neither woman moved, nor made a sound. Then, grandfather swung open the door and thundered into the kitchen where grandmother stood, frozen. It was clear that his mistress had told him of the encounter at the store. He had on his face a look altogether familiar. The house itself and all the things accumulated there, all that had henceforth never seen the man, seemed to shrink back, aghast. Without a word he grabbed grandmother in his hands and wrenched her out of the house and into the warm street.

He stopped at the corner, where building construction was going on. There, he began to beat her with his hands. My mother had followed him and fought to stop him, trying to tear him off her mother's crumpled body, but he was out of control and flung her off. It was only when grandmother lost consciousness that he let up. He stood over her for a moment, panting, before turning and leaving. My mother was crying, beside herself with panic and terror.

Just a few feet away, the open door of their home poured dim yellow light into the street. Alone, my mother dragged her mother, mangled beyond recognition, back into the house. She laid her in bed and began feverishly to treat her wounds with hot and cold compresses. She trembled, but her mother made no motion. She knew that in all her frenzy of activity she was only waiting for her mother to wake, to move again, to respond.

She sat up through the night nursing grandmother. After the commotion of the encounter and of her own irrepressible sobs, which had long since ceased, the room seemed uncannily quiet and the house around her strangely still. All of their two years residence, all of the progress they made away from grandfather, was obliterated in one blast. Grandmother, too, was still. Mother waited for the softly breathing body to wake, to speak, so that together they could rekindle the little motions and the warm talk that every day before had assured her that their little home held a life that thrived. After eight long hours, grandmother finally shuddered into consciousness, blinking her eyes open and closed, and not saying a word. Her voice had been knocked out of her, and it seemed she could only lift and drop her head very slightly, as if in resignation.

My mother wondered what could be done, and it seemed there was no answer. There was no one to help them. Her sister was studying in Japan. So was her older brother. She felt paralysis creeping into her, so that she could not think, could not hope. She held her mother on her lap and cried bitterly to God, asking, "My God, what have you done? How could you let this happen to us?"

A month passed. Grandmother continued to lie in bed without speech and without motion. My mother distracted herself from the severity of the situation by submitting utterly to its demands. She found that enduring it simply meant living it. Grandmother's incapacitation required mother to become the primary earner for the household. Her days were fuller than they had ever been. She tended to grandmother as best she could, while attending school and working odd jobs. But it was soon clear that she could not continue to maintain all her obligations, especially since the family no longer had a source of income. Unable to keep up with school-work, mother took a leave of absence. She began searching for a job and, with the help of her church pastor, was able to secure a position as teacher in a local elementary school, where she worked during the day. In the evenings, she took classes at a typing school nearby.

At last, after three months of rest and recuperation, grand-mother's condition gradually improved. Little by little she reas-sumed her daily routine. She began by taking short walks through the rooms, where the walls and objects she had not seen since the incident seemed to greet her warmly, and to enliven in her pres-ence. As the days passed she took on more and more responsibili-ties, cooking meals and tending to the household while my mother was working. Her strength returned, and then her voice, and with these the easy busyness and movement of home. The suspension that had held their lives frozen was broken through, and mother and daughter found that three months had been gained, three blessed months of progress. Again, they left the past behind them, and resumed.

After her recovery, grandmother began to rent out the extra rooms to college students studying in Seoul to supplement the household income. She was still too weak to leave the house to work. Meanwhile, mother's typing skills improved rapidly, and she was asked to serve as a teacher in her typing school. Then, another job offer came from Chosun Press Corporation for a typist, and my mother became, very suddenly, a young professional business woman. The changes in those years of her life came in violent lurches, but she rode them and mastered them with grace.

Protestant Christianity was introduced in Korea by mission-aries when my grandmother was a young woman. They taught her gospel stories that moved her to belief. I admire my grandmother for her belief, because young women especially at the time were pummeled into submission to Confucian models of behavior and thought. Its decrees were to be wholeheartedly obeyed. I imagine it must have been easier merely to accept the common mold of life than to decide for oneself. My grandmother must have possessed a great deal of courage and self-knowledge to know her own mind and to choose her own faith.

The moral education provided by Confucian family life was normal fare for young people. Respect for one's elders, parents, and nation was indoctrinated into young minds and enforced all through life. The goal of this education was to teach each person know his or her place. Every individual was assigned a static role and a hierarchical position in the family group, and in society. Absolute deference and an essentially religious devotion to patriarchy were at the center of the Confucian belief system. This doctrine and the ritual practices of ancestor veneration were at odds with the Christian faith, which prohibited the worship of idols and false gods.

Thus, as a member of a Confucian society, grandmother had to conceal her faith from the detection of others. Before she was married, my grandmother and all other single women like her were forbidden from leaving their homes without supervision. Women who defied these conventions earned bad reputations, and were often accused of having loose morals. If grandmother was caught breaking out of her confines, she would be beat about the legs—the common punishment of the time—and sent to live in exile with distant relatives. But my grandmother continued to pursue her belief. Her faith developed quickly and with vigor, and she nourished it with great resourcefulness, often sneaking out of the house to attend church. She memorized the teachings of the missionaries and worked to live according the bible's instructions.

Grandmother married in the typical way, through a matchmaker, at a typical age, 16. She played the role of a typical housewife, and bore the abuse of a philandering husband, a plight that was typical, too. Her marriage became a prison, enforced by colluding Korean customs that dictated that a man had every right. But my grandmother's faith sustained her. All of her suffering she offered up to God, and God colored it anew. It meant more than bearing her fair share. Her faith assured her that her suffering was for something, that it was a blessing.

When grandmother finally made the choice to overstep the limits of her role and leave her husband, she obtained a freedom such as she had never felt. She claimed a liberty unlicensed by her culture. This personal freedom in the midst of a nation oppressed captivated grandmother's children, and they accepted the faith of their mother. My mother came to the Christian faith the night her mother was beaten. Frightened for her mother's life, she spent the night pouring herself into prayer, and God answered her with grandmother's recovery.

In the face of this hardship and suffering, my mother and grandmother survived, fragile in some ways, but prevailing in others. No one and no circumstance could defeat their strong faith, even if they could imprison them as women in culturally-acceptable ways.

BROTHER'S DEATH

In Japan, my mother's elder sister married a tall, handsome graduate of Yonsei University. He came from a large family that adhered to strictly traditional Confucian ideals, which assigned value based on gender and rank of birth. As a Chul-ga Wai-in, my aunt was initiated into the family of her husband, to which she was expected to re-devote her life and her life's allegiance. A Chul-ga Wai-in is a woman in marriage who becomes an outsider to her own biological family, and is passed into the possession of her husband's families, to which her Confucian duties were transferred. This meant she was expected to produce sons for her husband's family, in order that the patriarchal system might continue. This also meant she could not return to her mother's home for anything more than short, periodic visits. Her husband, however, was a generous, warm man who did not exact every advantage that was his right under this system. In fact, he grew close to my grandmother and mother, to whom he became like another son and brother. Unfortunately, he and his wife now belonged to another family.

So it was that my grandmother "lost" her oldest daughter to marriage, leaving her with only her son and two daughters on whom she could depend in the event of hard times. But she did not lose my mother, even during the Second World War when the

Japanese began their horrific practice of rounding up young Korean women and herding them into brothels on the front line of for the uses of the Japanese soldiers. Many of these women found in marriage a guaranteed exemption from forcible service. But my mother was able to escape this fate even though she was not married because she was working for a Japanese company.

Still, mother struggled to make enough money to support herself, her mother, and her elder brother and sister who were both studying at universities in Japan. She was now the sole earner of her family, and each time tuition payments were due, she lost sleep scouring her mind for ways to come up with the money. Only faith and prayer sustained her. She only asked that she could endure until her brother completed his studies and returned to Korea.

My uncle was soon to graduate. At that time, this was an achievement that would bring distinction to the entire family and its name. Like his father, he had grown to be a handsome, impressive young man, though one out of step with contemporary expectations. He felt strongly about his responsibility to become a man unlike his father, of whose actions he deeply disapproved. He was emphatically gentle, endowed with a wonderful capacity for empathy. He loved my mother especially. As the eldest son, his loyalty ought to have belonged to his father. His deliberate avoidance of the man was an audacious display of his allegiance to my mother, and to the women of his family. However, this enforced avoidance meant that he was usually absent when situations with Grandfather arose.

The prospect of her brother's graduation filled mother with pride for his accomplishments, and, perhaps even more so, with hope for her own. Once she no longer had to work to pay her brother's tuition, she would have the chance to enter a program of study herself. Her brother often assured her, "After I graduate, it's your turn, Yun-ae. Then, I will support you." He was not the kind to repeat the popular saying, "When a woman gets married, that is the end of her." Uncle invested much of his own hope in the education of his sister.

At last, his final semester arrived. It was winter, and the weather was ferociously cold. One night, after returning from a prayer meeting, mother found a telegram tacked to the front door. It must have arrived in her absence. Taking it into her gloved hands and shutting the door against the wind, she saw that it had traveled a long way from Japan. With trembling fingers, she fumbled it open, and read the bold printed news that her brother was critically ill in a Japanese hospital. He had contracted a severe lung disease in the stress and strain of his studying, and the brutal weather had only exacerbated his poor health. My mother left straightaway for Tokyo's agonizing cold. She spent the journey with her eyes shut, pleading in groans and whimpers to God, spinning a snarled line of hope and entreaty to span her progress from home to her brother's bedside. She arrived, battered by winds. At the hospital, late in the night, she found that her brother had already died. She had come too late, and she had missed him. She stayed only long enough to catch her breath, and then returned alone, winding back up the line of hope as she traced her way back home. She had prayed so fiercely and without ceasing since she had read the telegram. She had had such hope for him, but God had not answered her prayers. Less than two weeks later, Seoul National University wrote accepting his application for a professorship in their Engineering School.

MARRIAGE

After Uncle's death, the family lived the rest of the winter as though it wouldn't end. The suddenness of their loss had struck like thunder and toppled over their accumulated hopes. The lives of each member of the family were entwined so intricately that each was bound up in the happiness and success of the others. What one lost, they all lost. My mother mourned her brother's loss—his lost future, his lost prospects—as well as her own. The women had depended on the eldest son to be their foundational support, to lead the family not only financially, but also in vision, especially as Grandmother aged. After suffering the violence that Grandfather had wielded as though it were an entitlement, they knew what it meant to be at the mercy of a man in a society that gave few rights to women. Uncle's death meant that the family of women no longer had any socially viable defenses. They had to realign, to reconsider the expectations they had fostered for their lives, and to take precautions.

The end of winter finally came, and once again the women found, with some amazement, that they had endured it, and that it had passed. But it seemed another winter was coming again. Because she needed to support Grandmother financially, mother could not begin her studies. Her youngest sister left home to teach at a woman's high school in Beijing, leaving mother and Grandmother alone in the emptied house.

The distress of the family coincided with that of their nation. The Japanese still ruled the country, and continued their forcible recruitment of Korean men and women to fatten their war machine. Many Korean men were forced into hard labor in Manchurian mines and factories. Women were herded into brothels for Japanese soldiers. My mother, though ostensibly safe under the employment of a Japanese publishing company, nevertheless felt the threat of what seemed an insatiable and wholly unpredictable force. The only fortification a woman could secure against such a threat lay in her complete removal from the pool of unattached Korean women that the Japanese continually scoured. She could only achieve this in marriage.

At that time, mother tutored the child of a neighbor, who took a liking to her. She was aware of mother's predicament and offered to introduce her to a 26-year old businessman she had known for many years, and whose character she could vouch for. Korean custom dictated that respectable men must first earn the approval of the bride's mother before meeting his intended, and he managed to make a good impression on Grandmother and my eldest aunt. Both women urged my mother to enter into marriage. Her courtship with my father, under strain of necessity, had to be accelerated. In just a few months, without fanfare, they were married in a small ceremony on January 3, 1944, at the Kwang-Hee Moon United Methodist Church. Grandfather did not show up.

Although my mother's deep faith filled her life with a purpose that diverged from the purposes Confucian convention designated to women, she was nevertheless deeply rooted in a culture dominated by these conventions. Daily she balanced the freedom granted her by her faith with her obligations as a woman and young bride. My mother prayed to thank God for allowing her to elude the "Comfort Women" recruitment that subjected so many women to horrific abuses. It was God's grace that spared her and gave her a chance at the life she wanted. She prayed for her future even as she reflected back upon her 26 years of pain, the death of her brother, and the suffering of her mother, whom she now left alone. On the first night of her marriage, she wept for all she left behind.

II.

New Family

SAE DECK: THE NEW BRIDE IN THE CHANG FAMILY

IF YOU JOURNEY TO the southern province of Chulla Nam Do and drive south for another hour, you come to a small village called Bul-Kyo, nestled cozily among rice fields, where the villagers operate as one family. My paternal grandfather flourished there as the herbal medicine doctor for the village, and a prominent, well-known member of the community. He owned many rice fields and employed many of the villagers as seasonal workers during the summer. He paid his workers in the rice they harvested, which they could sell for money at the regional market place.

My paternal grandparents had six children, four sons and two daughters. Their residence was divided into three detached buildings on a large tract of land. There was an inner house, an outer house, and a worker's quarters, each enclosed by gates. Grandfather built a deck under the shade of a tree in the garden, where the family would spend the daylight hours when the weather was warm, eating, playing, resting, and fanning themselves in the heat. The large rice cookers in the kitchen (bu-uk) wafted fumes and warm, moist air into the garden and beneath the floors, to heat the home during winter (ondol).

The entire household stirred with anticipation for my mother's arrival. To welcome the new young bride from Seoul, the family held a festival to which the entire village was invited. She was received enthusiastically, and the family gave the city girl the nickname Seoul Aga, which means Seoul Baby. My mother worked conscientiously to fulfill her in-law's expectations, which meant serving the family assiduously. Perhaps the member most pleased to welcome the newcomer was the eldest and first daughter-in-law of the household, who had borne the brunt of the household labor since her own initiation into the family. A new sister-in-law would ease the weight of the workload. The lives of these recruited women consisted essentially of constant servitude to the family of their husbands, preparing meals, cleaning, caring for the children, and tending to all the other tasks traditionally regarded as "women's work."

Under Confucian tradition, each new daughter-in-law had the additional task of demonstrating her devotion to the parent in-laws in a ritual each morning, so that she began each day in an act of obedience and submission. My mother would wake in the dark hours before dawn, bathe, apply make-up and don a Han bok, a formal Korean dress. She would then wait outside the door of her in-laws' bedroom, listening for a stir from within, which was her signal to enter. Once inside, she would perform the morning's gesture of honor by kneeling and drawing her forehead to the ground in a full bow before her parents' bed. Afterward, the day's labor would begin. My mother would scurry in her full traditional dress back to her quarters where she put on the day's working clothes, then join her elder sister-in-law in the first meal preparation. My mother performed her Morning Bow for three weeks, after which her doting father-in-law told her she could stop.

Each day in the Chang household began early. As the newest daughter-in-law waited quietly outside the door of her parents' bedroom, the myriad workers in the servant's quarters were stirring out of sleep, rising to dawn and bracing themselves for the tasks of the long day. When the sun lit the land, motion broke out all around the house, breaking through the night's suspension. Men stacked rice and straw in the store house for later use in the kitchen's cooking fires. Women stirred soup and prepared rice in large pots atop kitchen fires, or fluttered around the house tending to various chores. White smoke like the motion's exhaust rose in a sliver from the chimney. The members of the family woke one by one, each in turn, and plunged into the rhythm of the day's activity.

Mother became an important piece of the family's grinding, rolling mechanism. She studied under her sister-n-law in the workings of the household, and performed chores under her tutelage. These tasks she arduously performed became her entire life. There was no electricity or plumbing in the house, so human hands filled in the necessary labor to keep the house running smoothly. The women were kept occupied with constant, crucial work. They woke early to prepare soybean soup and rice for the large family's first meal. No sooner would the breakfast's refuse and dishes be cleared than preparations for lunch would have to begin. After the family reunited to eat their second meal, the women again cleaned the kitchen, then busied themselves with the sewing and mending of the family's clothes. All the linens and clothes had to be hand-washed then hand-ironed.

There was more than enough work to go around, as well as ways to perform it. One traditional method of ironing required two women to lay the damp clothes on a smooth stone and beat the wrinkles out with wooden bats. My mother had never seen this method enacted before, and watching her sister-in-law take a bat to the day's labor gave her considerable pleasure. One day, my mother asked her sister-in-law if she could have a try at it.

Her sister-in-law replied, "No! You've never tried it before, and it's not easy work. It takes skill, and rhythm. You might get hurt, or hurt someone else."

My mother's sister-in-law, having lived in the house longer and suffered her toil alone during her first months in the Chang family, took pride in her expertise. She had earned it. But my mother persisted, and her sister-in-law finally relented.

Whack! Whack! Whack! Whack! She beat the rhythm only shakily at first, but soon, joined by her sister-in-law, found a steady cadence. Beating the clothes together in the heat, sweating over their task, the two sisters were joined in a bond of shared work. The echo of their sisterly rhythm resounded throughout the house.

Marriage had extricated my mother so suddenly from the seedling life she and her mother had built to fullness in Seoul after leaving Grandfather. She now felt, waking each morning to new responsibilities, new people, and new prospects, the truth in the common saying that once the woman is married, she becomes an outsider to her own family (Chul-ga Wai-in). My mother knew that her marriage had initiated her into a new stage of her life as a woman. She left her mother to whom she had been so devoted, and now belonged to the family of her husband.

With this new stage came a new home, and new comforts. On restless nights, my mother could hear, echoing through the still house, the voice of her father-in-law reciting passages from the works of Mencius and Confucius. The sure, steady flow of his voice seemed to envelop her and all the others that lay slumbering, breathing in and out to his rhythms. She had come to belong to them, and she trusted that her husband's family would care for her as one of their own. Into grandfather's soft chant, my mother mingled her own prayers. She prayed for herself, for the life she would share with her husband. She promised to serve him with her life, and she prayed for her mother, far away in Seoul, who now slumbered in her home alone.

HURT FINGER

On market day, Grandfather and his foreman prepared their carts to make the journey to market, where they would purchase enough food and household essentials to sustain the family. On one day in particular, Grandmother made a special request. She knew it was the season for Go-Mak (a type of clam) and that it would be the top-selling fare at today's market.

The regional market system was the economic life-blood of the region. The location of the gathering would move from town to town and village to village according to the season and the day of the month, to distribute the hardship of travel among the region's residents. Vendors and buyers would gather in a common location to exchange their products, then part again in the evening, each bearing a new load of goods bought and money earned.

This was the first time my mother, the family's Seoul Aga, had even heard of such a market. It thrilled her to imagine so many men from villages speckled throughout the countryside, like pieces of a splintered city, convening together to talk and barter and exchange what they had produced. In Seoul, people were smashed elbow to elbow all the time, but never met each other's eyes. They coexisted but never converged. Here, people depended on each other. These men toiled in the earth and caught things with their hands, then tendered the results of their labor to others, hand to hand. My mother knew that, had she been a man, she herself could tramp through the out-sprawled country to the market, where she would join in that crucial noise and activity of exchange, and look into the faces of the men she had never seen before. But the market was a long way off, and women were not invited to accompany the men. The women of the household didn't even think of it. They had their realm, and they remained enclosed there, within the walls of the home. Housework was the first and only task. So as the men assembled, the women busied themselves with their own responsibilities, and waited.

Grandfather and his workers returned early, towing down the lane carts overflowing with new acquisitions. To prepare for the feast, mother's sister-in-law began boiling water in a large Ka Ma Sot, a black rice cooker or kettle. This was the first my mother had ever seen of the little shelled creatures, each the size of a man's thumb and caked with mud from the bottom of the sea. After scrubbing the muck from their surfaces, mother's sister-in-law sprinkled salt on the Go-Mak to tease their shells apart so she could give them a more thorough clean. The little creatures bloomed open like sea flowers, their curved shell showing a lustrous gray-blue, like a sky seen from underwater. Sister-in-law dumped the Go-Mak into the large black iron pot. The little opened shells shut when they touched the boiling water. She then stirred them in one direction with a large wooden spoon that was the width of a man's forearm, so the meat would stick to one side of the shell.

Meanwhile, my mother prepared the sauce. She minced fresh garlic and scallions, roasted sesame seeds, and stirred them into a base of soy sauce and aromatic oil. Her hands were quick. She performed her task with pride. Practice had made her skillful. As she worked, she glanced back at the mountain of fresh Go-Mak, and wondered how the family could possibly consume so much.

Drawn to the gurgling pot by the familiar aroma, the family members began to gather. The women poured the steaming Go-Mak into a large bowl placed in the center of the patio. Go-Mak was a special favorite of the children. They scuttled in nearest to the bowl and sucked in the steam, their faces bobbing over the rim. Confucian custom dictated that the men eat first, starting with the oldest and proceeding to the youngest. The women came next, in age order, and then, finally, the daughters-in-law. After dousing them in sauce, my mother and her sister-in-law pried open the Go-Mak for the others by pulling apart the shells with their two thumbnails. They had to take care to catch the milk-white liquid that dripped from the opened shells—it was a special delicacy. Uncles, aunts, elders, nieces, and nephews all gathered around, waiting to be fed. The process was arduous, so each bite was relished. My mother managed to set aside a plate for her father-in-law, arranging the shells carefully and covering them in the sauce she had made.

After all the members of the family ate their fill and wandered off, glutted and drowsy, she was invited to have her first taste. She ate slowly, first examining the fleshy insides of the blue-mouthed shell, breathing in the smell, and then rolling the Go-Mak juice, smooth as cream soup, across her tongue. The old ritual in which she now had a part enchanted her. The entire day had been a procession of fresh sights and sensations, and she savored their newness. She would remember the day for the rest of her life. She ate until she too was glutted.

The day passed, and evening came. As the excitement of the day waned, a pain that become more and more acute began to prickle in my mother's hands. By sunset, her thumbs had swelled so they looked like little pink sausages. Tiny iridescent shards of the Go-Mak shells had pierced through the tender skin of her thumbs. By the next morning she had developed a fever. Her mother-in-law took one look at her Seoul Aga, and instantly knew the cause. She applied a traditional salve of soy sauce and soy bean past to my mother's thumbs. For the remainder of the six month she spent in the household, my mother was not permitted to lift a finger. Those months were happy ones. Even though Confucian convention treated women harshly at times, it also showed great care to its weaker ones.

STILLBIRTH

After spending the first six months of their marriage in the country, my mother and father returned to Seoul, eager to begin an independent life of their own. They found a house in the city's suburbs with space for the large family they intended, and settled down. But the atmosphere in Seoul had worsened since my mother had left for the country, where the family had been isolated from the effects of the Japanese presence.

The year was 1945, a tense time in Seoul. Korean contempt for the occupying Japanese had grown intense, and a warlike intent began to brew among the discontented, with the object of eradicating the Japanese presence. Strapped for labor resources, the Japanese had begun to draft young Korean men to fight for the Japanese cause in Manchuria and in the Shantung provinces, a callous move that only roused the indignation of the people. Such were the conditions that the enmity between the two Asian nations, while it has diminished over time, rankles still to this day. Stripped bare by the Japanese, the country could no longer yield enough food to feed its own people. Strict rationing of all supplies and food meant that together, the Korean people had to eke sustenance out of very little. The entire nation was forced to subsist on a diet of potatoes and barley. Rice was hardly ever available. Only through extreme thrift were the people able to manage. Living no longer meant the things it ought to have meant. Life shed its luster and showed bare bones. The essential, only thing was to survive.

At the time my father served at the general affairs office of the Japanese army, and was thus saved from the draft that wrenched other men from their homes. His privileged position occasionally allowed him to procure small rations of rice for his family, but at the price of a night's lost sleep. My father knew his association with the Japanese earned him his security, and gave him a bit of privilege over his countrymen.

Soon after their arrival in Seoul, my mother learned she was pregnant. But her meager diet had weakened her so severely that she could no longer bear to eat more than small morsels, which were not enough to sustain her and the baby. She seemed to shrink in size, even as the baby grew inside her. She expended all of her strength merely fighting to live, to function, so that there was none left to impart to her child. One month after he was born, my brother died. My mother's grief aggravated her already compromised physical condition. She and her husband faced their first loss, the first joint sorrow of their lives together. The entire nation seemed to mourn with them for its own billion losses, all the myriad sacrifices the living had to make to endure.

My mother's hopes, like the hopes of her fellow Koreans, were set on liberation. The nation waited together for the relief that would release them all. In murmurs exchanged behind closed doors, they comforted themselves with assurances. "We shall be independent and liberated soon," they said. That day finally came. On August 15, 1945, Korea won its liberation from Japanese occupation after two generations of oppression. For thirty six years the Japanese had suppressed the personality and will of the nation. All of life had been enduring, bearing. Now that the constraints had been lifted, Koreans no longer knew what to do with the prospect of new life spread open in front of them. The trauma of their captivity had induced in them a kind of amnesia. They did not remember what normalcy was, what it entailed, or how to return to what had been. They had to re-learn life and how to want things again. General disorder and confusion swept the country. The nation hesitated at the threshold of its new chance.

In the midst of the nation's bewilderment, my mother's second pregnancy ended in a stillbirth. My sister died in the womb. Mother was devastated. She and Father had returned to Seoul with such a store of hope, but their two failed pregnancies had expended the last of it. She had had the audacity to expect, to ask something of life, and it had denied her again.

My mother felt the distinct shame of being a wife who could not bear her husband a child. Maternity was such a crucial rite of passage for Korean women. Confucian convention demanded that a woman produce offspring for her husband and his family. But perhaps, especially in this moment in the nation's history, what became even more elemental for Korean women was not just that they generate life, but that they suffer it. In a society in which men went out into the world, earned, and acted, women were relegated to a kind of enforced passivity. Women suffered. They endured. They swallowed life down. Life happened to them. How deeply, how utterly it did. Men claimed the right to make decisions and to fight wars, but women were the ones to bear the consequences. They were the ones to mourn when their men died. They were life's keepers. All the blows that fate delivered, all the nation endured, all they ever experienced stood whole and sealed in their very souls, in the marrow of their bones. My mother had witnessed her own mother suffer, and now she came to know suffering in her own turn. It was Han-sorrow, grief that a woman feels in her bones. This sorrow consumed her, and she felt in it the sorrow of her mother, and of all the women of her culture. My mother had failed to give life, but now she suffered it as she never had before. Never in her 26 years had something reached to such depths in her. It consumed her so she no longer had strength to make decisions for her own future. Her faith died within her.

She let her husband decide the next step. Their attempt at creating a new life had failed, and he determined that they should go back to the embrace of his hometown. So they disposed of their life in Seoul and returned to Bul-Kyo.

HOPE

When a woman marries in Korea, she is expected to give birth to a son. Confucian convention dictates that it is the most important task of womanhood. The son was the link that connected one generation to the next. A family grew around its men. Women were lost and acquired, taken from the family of their birth to join that of their husbands. Families with many sons gained in their marriages women to labor and live under their name, backs to share the load of the housework. Thus, women who bore sons fortified full family lines. My mother knew what was expected of her, and because she loved her husband and his family, she wanted to grant them their hopes and fulfill her duty to them.

My mother returned to the large household of her husband's family having failed to do her duty, and found herself the subject of constant talk and the object of unrelenting solicitude. Her mother in law continually asked her whether she was too weak to bear children. Her father-in-law, the Chinese medicine doctor, prescribed her innumerable medications to prime her body for impregnation. Well-meaning neighbors happened by, offering condolences and gave advice. Every warning, every suggestion my mother heeded faithfully, as though each would heal her, each would bring success. Since her return to the village, her sole desire, her sole task had been to bear a child for her husband. Hope had long since flagged in her, so she turned to that of others, which overflowed in endless, urgent supply on her behalf.

One especially persistent neighbor invited mother to pray with her in a special place beyond the village, where they could cry out their prayers alone. My mother agreed to follow her, and they trekked together beyond the house and through the fields. As they walked, the neighbor instructed: "Keep walking; never look over your shoulder." Mother obeyed. She would do anything that might work, believe any superstition that might implant the spark of hope back into her heart. Every inch of her, body and soul, was possessed by an exhaustion she couldn't shake. She couldn't help but feel that something inside her had become irreversibly compromised.

The two women reached the clearing, and they settled down to pray. My mother's faith had withered after her stillbirth, and she had turned her heart from prayer. God never seemed to answer in the way she hoped and deserved. But, kneeling now with her face pressed into her knees, she felt again the lure of the old, embracing intimacy. Perhaps it wasn't hope but desire alone that had grown so fierce that she could no longer resist the asking, the pleading that had failed so many times before. The old channel burst into life again, and she began to cry out her pent-up prayers. She prayed for the life of a new child, for her mother, and for her mother-in-law. She wept the loss of her brother, and the loss of her two children. Her sorrow seemed to crack open upon the mountains in the distance, and to echo finally away.

Each morning, instead of her Morning Bow, she returned to her seclusion to pray. Each time she heeded her neighbor's warning never to look back at what she had left behind. In prayer, mother was renewed. Each day she grew stronger. The efforts and schemes of others that had sustained her for months she replaced with her own. In her own voice, she prayed for what she wanted. In Chinese thought, from which much of the Korean world-view is derived, heart and mind are not sundered, but are denoted as a single functioning unit by the word "Shin" (which means "ultimate power"). Her own Shin resounded with resolution: "Whatever happens, I shall have my baby."

SO-DU-BANG-SOE

My mother delivered her third baby in the midst of noisy commotion. The entire family had joined the effort of the delivery. They would strive to save the baby at all costs. My maternal grandmother had traveled from Seoul to be present for the crucial birth, and both grandmothers prayed fervently to their separate gods. They all hoped for life.

After hours of labor and inflamed hope, I was born. Both grandmothers rose from their prayers to receive the baby upon the lid of a big iron cooking pot, a Korean tradition that ensured the child would live a long life. They called me So-Du-Bang-Soe, which means "baby delivered on the lid of an iron pot."

News of the successful delivery spread to the outer rooms where members of the family waited in suspense. Celebration erupted throughout the house for the new, sound life that had answered their hopes.

After three years of waiting, no one minded that the child that had finally come was not a boy. Grandfather chose the name Hwa-In from, Hwa means rice and In means compassionate heart and perseverance of mind. The family fulfilled in the hope that had burned in them for three years, fostered a new hope for the child—that she would grow in health, and that live to bring goodness to the world.

Every night, Grandfather recited prayers for the health of his daughter-in-law and her new child. Exhausted from the strain of labor, my mother rested in bed for months. However, her joy and the prayer and support of her husband's family nourished her body and soul. Each day she grew stronger.

III.

Mother of a Daughter

WOO AEA SA

AFTER KOREA'S LIBERATION, POLITICAL refugees who fled the country began to retrace their old paths of exile, returning home to cleared air and fresh prospects. A government-in-exile had been assembled in Shanghai, and the expatriate officials began trickling back to the old seat of the nation's government in Seoul. A new government was created under a new political system. The Dae Han Min Kuk (the Korean name for Korea) was born.

Mother's younger sister had left home to study embroidery in Tokyo. There, my aunt met a Korean man who also studied in Japan. The two married and settled in Beijing, where she taught at a school for girls. After Korea's liberation, she joined the long procession of the thousands of Koreans returning home, bringing with her fifty girl orphans who had lost their parents in the war. She established a house in Ssangrim Dong where the girls could live, and where she could teach them embroidery in her spare time. It was called Woo Aea Sa—woo for friend, aea for love, sa for house—the house of loving friends. Her life in Seoul, resumed after so long an absence, quickly opened and filled with new purpose. Her husband was appointed Vice Minister of Finance of the new Korean government, and together they took an active role in politics and the community.

My aunt's students took enthusiastically to their embroidering. The precision and creativity of the task gave them an outlet for their lives' frustrations. To sell the pieces they created, my aunt opened a small shop in Myung Dong. The profits provided tuition for the studies of the growing girls. As business grew, she asked mother to return to Seoul to take part in what she had created.

THE SOURCE OF LIFE

The history of the humanity proves that women were not always considered the lesser sex. Many cultures revered women as the ultimate ancestor of the human race, the womb from which life had first emerged. The male-dominated culture in which my mother now lived, however, seemed to have reduced women from a source of life to a mere means to achieve it. Life-making was the labor of women, and men arrogated more rights than responsibilities in the bearing and raising of their offspring.

But mother was proud of the life that had come from her, proud that she had been able to impart it. Her daughter was the single visible fruit of her 27 years, her life's bloom. It was as though, in motherhood, some essential spark in herself had taken its own shape, so that her own life now seemed to stand apart from her, in her daughter. She poured herself with relish into the maternity she had so long sought, into all the myriad tasks that caring for a little life required.

The fact that I depended on her made my mother strong. She became a women who cared arduously, with her whole being, for others. She helped her sister as much as she could with her education assignments, collecting the artwork of other embroiderers, and displaying and selling them so the artists could earn money for their work. Even in the general disorder that ensued after the

Japanese departed, people began to regain their wealth and embark upon business ventures that the stifling Japanese occupation had made impossible. People no longer had to scrimp and hoard. Their lives, which had contracted and stiffened to survive, began to unfurl again. Limbs and fingers uncurled. People wanted contact again, not only with each other, but with the generosity and variety of life that they had been denied.

Women too sought projects and purposes of their own. My aunt's store began to grow not only as a place of commerce but as a center of communication in which women could gather and open themselves to each other. Through their talk and through the art of embroidery, the women artists articulated their secret sorrows, spread them into shape and form.

Just as the nation was beginning to learn how to be free again, new conflict erupted. The Communist forces of North Korea and the People's Army roused the engines of war. They began stealthily to seize the families of South Korean government officials and to convey them into captivity in the North. My aunt's husband went into hiding, as did many others. Inexplicable fires broke out all over the city. News of the impending arrival of the North Korean Army arrested Seoul in panic. Once again, frightened for their lives, people scrambled to flee the country. My aunt's embroidery store, like so many of the new shops that had just entered their infancies, was torched, along with all the work accumulated there. The orphans' home was destroyed as well.

Then came the news that my uncle had been captured. The family endured its darkest time. My mother felt a sorrow that nothing could appease. It was as though she had lost her own husband. Everyone suffered. The men rushed to the battle field only to die or to be hurt. Women and children stayed behind.

In the midst of the turmoil, my mother and aunt experienced the singular bitterness of a war fought between armies of the same nation. Korean mothers, hardly recovered from the old affliction, again felt their fury pushed cheek-by-jowl against the fury of new war. With their prayers and their moaning they beat on heaven's door. They wanted justice, respite from suffering—all that they deserved but had never been granted. Heaven did not reply.

Mother evacuated to Pusan, the southern-most city. Beside my father, with her three-year-old So-Du-Bang-Soe strapped to her back, she hiked south, as bullets showered down from the sky.

NEW LIFE

A time of hardship instills a sense of discipline in those who can endure. In Pusan, mother set herself to this new chance arduously. She labored alongside her husband to get his new business off the ground, and did all she could to raise her daughter in the best way. She embodied the ideal of a good wife and a wise mother, and was praised by her neighbors for her generosity. Even though there was no financial need to do so, mother kept up her embroidery. She also prayed stubbornly for her husband who did not share her faith. Most of her effort, however, she invested in bringing me up to be a good and modest women.

"Hwain, it's not a good thing to work where your daddy sleeps."

"Hwain, when you sit down to take a meal, you must behave well."

"Hwain, you must not use bad words."

She proved to be a very traditional mother, instilling in me as best she could the moral values and dignity her mother had given her. She invested such hope in me, her only child, and motherhood seemed to have come when she needed it most. She only ever treated me with utmost patience, never breaking out into harsh words or revealing her anger, even if she was in a bad mood. My parents never argued in loud voices, nor fought in front of me. If they had something to discuss, it only reached me in soft mutterings through the walls at night.

She wanted to have a second child after I turned four, but her weak physical condition made it impossible. Unable to have another, she invested all her energy in the care of her only daughter, who had given her so much pain to bear. She never took her eyes off me, never missed a thing.

"Mom, there is a kindergarten here, too. I saw some kids passing by in the back street. They were wearing the same apron that I had when I went to kindergarten!" I had returned from the market with the maid one day, and I could see my mother was startled at the fact of my discovery. She had lied to me when we moved to Pusan—telling me there was no kindergarten nearby that I could attend—because she thought that our stay in the new city might only be temporary. She could not hide her delight in seeing how much her daughter had grown, even though it meant she could no longer lie to me to keep me safe.

The next day mother took me to Soo Jung Kindergarten and registered me at once. With her skillful hands she embroidered beautiful patterns on my school uniforms that made me proud to wear them. Even though ours was the smallest house on the corner of market place, she was proud of her station and all she and her husband had achieved. She wanted me to match up with the other children I met, to have no need of envy.

WEAK BUT STRONG

Evacuees from all of the country made the dangerous trek to Pusan. New faces eager to resume life filled the streets from the government building to the market place.

Mother's two sisters also settled in Pusan with their families. My eldest aunt lived in a big house with her husband, now the director of the city's customs office, their five sons, and their daughter. Younger aunt also relocated to the city with her three children and established a new orphanage and a new store to sell the girls' embroidery. Her enthusiastic involvement in her work distracted her from the loss of her husband.

Compared to her sisters, my mother had no advantages. She had never gone to college to get a degree, and had no opportunity to study abroad. She had been denied that opening of life that so many women her age had experienced when they left home, studied new things, and fell in love. Women who were educated shared between them a kind of camaraderie in which my mother could not partake. They belonged to Yonsei University or Ewha University alumnae clubs that threw parties for their members. Uncle would invite his fellow Yonsei graduates to his house, lit up with voices and laughter, where they'd carouse on into the night. My mother's younger sister also found her place in the society of Pusan. Government officials in the city who knew of her husband's capture supported her, and her business quickly prospered.

Mother often felt the sting of her own humble position in life. Her sisters seemed to have found so much more success. She took solace in her motherhood, and focused all of her attention and energy on me, for whom she was eager to lay down any sacrifice. My dependence made her strong by necessity. She devoted her hours to prayer, and soothed her frustrations with the conviction that God would take care of her and provide for all she could need.

My mother began to grow stronger in motherhood like a flower grows from its bud. She remembered an old man with long white hair that she once saw in her dream, and she was convinced he would guide and console her through the difficulties of her life. Her daughter became her secret hope.

A CHILD PICKED ON THE STREET

At the heart of Soo Jung dong, Pusan city, was the famous Jagalchi market stocked with goods combed from the nearby sea. All classes clashed and merged at the market, and, no matter how rich or poor, haggled for the lowest prices. The market was always in uproar: customers quibbled with vendors over prices; vendors battled each other for customers; fish fresh from the sea flapped saltwater into the briny air. A careless woman would cry out that her purse had been stolen, only to be drowned out by the persistent call of the vendors, shouting, "Come and see, it's a bargain!" Groups of orphans trouped somberly along the street bagging their day's finds, as young men delivering goods on their backs weaved through them, sighing heavily. In the pandemonium of the back streets, women in trunk pants bore bamboo basket on their heads brimming with wild edible greens, fresh vegetables, lively mackerels, or saucy pike, chanting "Just OOW for a lump." In between their bursts of shouting, they spoke to one another, laughing, fighting, and lamenting. Each had some grievance to tell, some story of the hard luck she had come upon in her life, and these softer words made a low song that joined them all together, and encompassed in it all the people who converged there at the marketplace.

"Is Hwain's mother at home?" said a voice outside the door.

"Yes, who's asking?" When my mother opened the door, she was surprised see the humble form of the superintendent of my kindergarten standing in the sun. My mother was happy to receive a visitor, and invited her in and served her hot tea and fruit. They spoke warmly about happenings in the school and her daughter's studies.

After a few minutes of enthusiastic talk, the superintendent grew quiet and grave. She had apparently come to discuss some serious matter, which she now prepared to broach. "Hwain's mother, please don't be offended. I must ask you something about your daughter." My mother wondered if I had done something wrong. The superintendent's sudden shift of mood agitated her, and she was eager to hear what the matter was so she could figure out how to best handle it. "Tell me now, it doesn't matter to me."

"It's something I heard it from Jungwon's mother," the woman hesitated. "People are saying that you found Hwain on the street, and took her in. Is that true?"

"What!? What is this all about?" Mother felt all her blood rise to her face.

The superintendent had to calm her and coax her to speak, before my mother finally collected herself and began to describe in full detail all the struggle of her failed pregnancies. She had not been able to conceive for years because of her frailty, until she was finally able to give birth to a daughter. Hwain was, in fact, her own child. The superintendent let out a sigh of relief. She explained her own concerns after having heard such a strange rumor, and her esteem for the child.

"I doubted it was true, seeing how affectionate you are with her. I just wanted to be sure. It's only because I like her so much."

The teacher and mother shared a relieved smile and closed their talk with cleared minds. Mother and the teacher parted ways silently, glad that they had come to an understanding. My mother could not believe that chatter could spread so maliciously, all because she had given birth so late.

BASHFUL MOTHER

Near us lived an old couple who had spent most of their lives in Japan. Mother called them Mr. and Mrs. Oh Sang. They became her dear friends. I called them aunt and uncle, because they treated me with such kindness, as though I were part of their family. They had no children of their own. Aunt Oh Sang, 15 years older than my mother, became her closest confidante and counselor.

"Hwain's mother! Let me see you," she said one day during one of her visits. "I heard it through the grapevine that Hwain's father remarried. Is that true?"

"What are you talking about? I don't understand!" Mother answered with surprise.

"Well, I heard from Mrs. Kim that Hwain's father said he bought a mirror to give to his new bride. I was shocked. It's been said that you are the new bride and that Hwain is a foster child. Is that true?"

My mother was shocked. Her husband liked to make jokes, but they had never before been taken as truth. She was infuriated with him for spreading rumors that the entire town apparently believed. She explained bitterly to Mrs. Oh Sang that the superintendent of the kindergarten had also visited and asked about a rumor that her husband had carelessly spread. She was ashamed.

That evening, as soon as my father got home, mother scolded him severely and told him in detail what the people in town had been saying about their family. My father laughed the whole story through. He scoffed at the sensitive nerves of his wife.

"How can you embarrass your wife and daughter?" My mother demanded. But her husband did not admit fault, and she had to seethe out her frustrations alone.

When I entered elementary school, my mother made one-piece dresses for me and aprons embroidered with hearts. She made a name tag for me that read: 1–1 Chang, Hwain because I belonged to the first class of the first grade. On my first day, the teacher asked me to call my mother in for a meeting. I took her by the hand and led her into the school. Many children and their parents were standing about, preparing for the entrance ceremony. When we found my teacher, she led us to the office of the principal.

"Are you Hwain's mother?" he asked.

"Yes, I am."

"I have chosen Hwain to deliver the opening remarks for today's ceremony. I asked her to practice for me, and she read it several times through perfectly, and even memorized the entire thing. I asked her to bring her parents so I could let you know I've chosen her." She could hardly hear the president's commendation, heart was pounding so powerfully. She was so flustered that she left the room without properly thanking the principal.

The entrance ceremony was held as expected. Students dressed in bright colors and their parents gathered and greeted one another. But my mother was silent and pale. She hoped that I'd do well, that I'd make no mistakes. She was so nervous for me that she couldn't bear to watch or listen, and hid herself beneath a tree in the corner of the school grounds. I was only a first grader and had never spoken in public. She did not emerge until I finished, and she heard the applause.

My mother received endless compliments and congratulations. She had not heard a single word of my valedictory, but tears filled her eyes. She was so proud at what I had accomplished.

From her youngest years she grew up wedged between her older sister and younger sister, always having to yield to one or the other. She had grown up revering her brother and fearing her father. She never had the stature or command of any of them, and had grown expecting perhaps too little from herself. But now she found confidence in what I, a small girl, had achieved. She was so impressed by that she didn't know what to do with all the delight that brimmed from her.

In her heart she said: "Dear God, thank you. I will raise her well. I will do my best." Then she began to look for me in the crowd.

THE LOVE OF A MOTHER

My mother had two more miscarriages after me. She couldn't hold a child for more than two months in her womb. They spilled out of her in a mass of blood. She so wanted to deliver a son, but it began to seem impossible given her body's weakness. Her husband continued to pressure her to give him a son, and the neighbors derisively referred to me as an only daughter.

My mother grew tired of living near a market. The noise often became oppressive. She soon decided to move to a new town—Daesin Dong—for my sake. I transferred to Daesin elementary school. It was not easy to leave a loving teacher and friendly neighbors, but my mother made the choice to do what was best for my future. I was eight and in the second grade. Because she could deliver no new child into the world, my mother devoted a powerful, pent-up love to me, her sole child. She remembered her own childhood and how she had suffered, and made every effort to secure a better life for me. But she got weaker by the day. Her limbs grew slimmer every day, and her face became haggard. She refused to take any medical exams and worked for us without complaint.

"Hi, Driver, would you please drive her to school today?" Mother asked our private car driver to bring me to school, without telling father. It was raining that day and she didn't want me to have trouble walking on the muddy street. She prepared breakfast and dressed me hurriedly, and pushed me out the door toward the driver who awaited me.

Not knowing my mother's intentions, I scurried off to school. I bid the driver good morning.

"Oh! Hwain, come on, get on it," he said, and began to take me the way to school.

"Driver, I want to get off here." I said.

"You don't want me to take you all the way?" he asked.

"No, I'd better get off here. I feel sorry for other kids. Everybody walks to school, and I don't want to go alone." I got out of our car far from school.

"Why does mom want to me ride to school? It's embarrassing!" I mumbled. I didn't understand that she was only showing me her love.

IDEAL MOTHERHOOD

My mother filled out her role as a mother and housewife. She worked arduously to create the perfect home for her husband and daughter. Her life revolved around her service to us; in the mornings she rose the earliest to dress and apply make-up, then prepared a beautiful spread for our breakfast. When we finished, she accompanied my father to the door, helped him put on his coat and shoes, and saw him off at the gate. While we were away from home during the day, my mother prepared our meals. She was an amazing cook and always set before us steaming dishes that surprised and delighted us. She had a housekeeper to reduce the load of the family's cleaning and washing, but she always went to the market to buy her own ingredients for the meals she so painstakingly prepared. At night, she was the last to go to bed.

Even though they weren't a particularly affectionate or demonstrative couple, my parents discussed every issue, although my mother usually yielded to her husband's choices. My mother was bound to my father by responsibility rather than love. My father was not different from other men in his situation in that he spent most of his day away from his home, working long hours from day to night. In the evenings, he went out to bars with coworkers, to keep up with the social aspect of his business, where he drew the interest of women. My mother did not want to raise her temper to her husband, or to try and exact any restrictions on his behavior, because it was not likely that he would submit. Rather, she tried to maintain his interest in his life at home, with his family. She felt it was her role to keep the family sound.

My mother had witnessed in her childhood a marriage in which all parties suffered. She had developed in her heart a hope for a happy, simple family life in which all members supported each other. She wanted to do whatever she could to give herself and her family a good life together. So she did whatever she felt a good mother and wife ought to do. Her own life and the reach of her influence were decidedly bounded in scope. She was not as socially active as her sisters, and spent her days treading the same ground, the same paths back and forth, to the market or to her daughter's school or to the homes of her few relatives, then back home. However, she treated each day as though it held promises, new lessons to be learned. Her eyes were always open, and she learned from every interaction, every observation. At parent-teacher meetings held in her daughter's school, she watched the other parents to see what their own lives were like, and how they treated their children. She took care to form the right relationships with her daughter's teachers, so that she could make sure her daughter was well-looked after when she was at school.

Perhaps the only thing she did solely for herself was the embroidery that had become important to her as an assertion of her individuality, of what she could create alone, apart from others. She even sold some of her pieces and tutored young girls to earn her own pocket money and to contribute to the family's income. Her communication with the materials, the thread, the needles, the colors was the purest she had ever experienced. All the secrets she found impossible to express, simply because there were no words and no people to tell, she spoke, stitch by stitch, into her embroidery.

Her two sisters who had also fled to Pusan had already succeeded economically. Her eldest sister's husband had bought a big house for his big family. I remember visiting and eating dinner around an enormous table piled with delicacies, with my five cousins battling for the biggest portions. My mother's younger sister had also found success in her embroidering store, and returned to

Seoul to extend her business. My mother was always thankful that her sisters were blessed with such prosperity, and was eager to help them whenever they asked.

My father was the second born of six brothers and sisters, who remained in the country with Grandfather. Only father's youngest sister, whose husband worked for a bank in Pusan, lived nearby. Mother served her husband's parents and siblings faithfully, even organizing large family events for special occasions. My grandparents often visited our home. I still remember the way he would sit cross-legged at the head of my bed, reciting a sutra for my health and future fortune. Praying in time with grandfather's rhythmic recitation always brought joy to my mother.

DOLL HOUSE

Ten years passed since the liberation of the country and the disaster of the Korean War (June 25, 1950). As the country stabilized in the midst of these changes, women too transitioned into new phases of cultural identity. The introduction of western ideas began to stretch the role of woman to more than their traditional relegation to solely domestic realms. Women began to work, and to earn. My mother began a business doing embroidery and making dolls in Seoul. There, she hired many of the young girls from the ages of 15 to 20 who had come to Seoul from all over the country in search of jobs. These women worked with her to produce dolls and lived together. While managing her factory workers, she also taught embroidery classes to women either to learn bankable skills.

In the day, the large factory room housed both experienced workers and young women who had just begun their employment. The room was split in the middle, with the newcomers at one end spinning thread and cutting silk threads for the craftswomen to use in their embroidery. Their work provided the craftswomen with materials for production, and accustomed them to the process of embroidery. First, they unwound thread from reels and fixed them onto embroidery boxes with a pin. Then they divided the long, unwound thread into three separate lines. Each line was wetted with spit, then twisted between the palms. The three separate lines were then twisted into one strand. The twisting and tightening of the strands creates strong and shiny silk thread. When completed, the thread was given to the craftswomen, who embroidered the colored lines into beautiful shapes on silk cloth. They created the shapes of the four gracious plants, the Mae, Nan, Kuk, and Chuk, the Korean apricot blossom and orchid, the chrysanthemum, bamboo tree and symbolic shapes of roses. The traced cranes, and stiched the words "Bok," meaning blessing, and "Soo," to live long. The embroidery was then sold to various markets and stores.

Beside the embroidery room was another large room in which the dolls were made. A large table spanned the length of the room. The workers sat on both sides of the table, each performing a specific task, adding detail to each doll. One women drew the eyes and make up on the faces, another attached the hands, another the legs. The dolls could be given hair of almost any color, arranged in all kinds of styles. Some faces had big western eyes, others were painted with smaller, oriental eyes. There were little girl dolls and lady dolls too. Sitting, standing, and dancing dolls were each positioned according to its story. These were all placed in plastic bags and sent to stores to be sold.

Each worker was paid according to the hours she worked and her rank in the factory hierarchy. However hard these women worked, the money they earned was by no means their own. They had sick mothers, brothers in school, family in other parts of the country to support. Women charged with the traditional role of the family's keeper began to fulfill their responsibilities economically. The women who worked for my mother bore their responsibility to their families gravely and with fortitude. Mother's doll house became a place where women gathered to work productivity out of need. Each suffered her own disappointments, each had homes, hearts of sorrow to which they were connected out in the rest of the country, and cried for their families every night. The women took comfort in the Han they all felt so fiercely, and which they shared. My mother took care of these women, and shared in their sorrows.

IV.

As a Strong Woman

YANGLIM'S MOTHER

FROM VERY EARLY IN the morning our two bathrooms were constantly brimming with people washing up for the day. People lined up at the water stand near the kitchen to wash their faces and brush their teeth, each rushing along so the others could get their turn. Preparations for breakfast began immediately. Soup made from dried radish leaves tingled in the noses of the rising workers and made their stomachs growl. Everybody gathered around the breakfast table where bowls of rice and soup awaited them. Chopsticks flickered back and forth from the plates of kimchi placed here and there. Mother always wished she could provide her workers with a hardier meal, but there were so many mouths to feed, and our own family unit to support with money left over after the wages were paid.

When winter came, mother bought hundreds of cabbages to make enough kimchi to last us for months. We used the leftover cabbage in all kinds of soups to feed the hungry mouths of the household.

One day a woman we didn't know came to the house and asked to speak to mother. A worker invited her in and she began to pour out her story. "My husband is a drunkard and he abuses me. His habit is getting worse and I'm worried for my life. I left the house because I couldn't take it anymore. Would you let me stay in your house?"

My mother carefully considered whether she could support this woman in need. Money was already tight because of all the tenants we housed and fed. The woman was not young, and seemed fragile to endure the long hours in one of the work rooms.

"Can you help with kitchen work?" she asked.

"Yes, of course I can," said the woman gratefully. "But, I have one more thing to ask. I have a daughter who must stay with me. Can she live here too?" My mother hesitated. There was scarcely enough space and resources in the house to support its current capacity of workers. But my mother had to relent; she couldn't turn a mother and her daughter away.

Yanglim's mother proved to be a hard worker, and was soon initiated into the embroidery and doll rooms. Her daughter was 14 years old. Mother asked Yanglim's mother to treat the other children as she did her own daughter. She was worried that she would give more food to Yanglim than the others.

The arrival of Yanglim's mother meant that the Oksoo Chung, who was in charge of errands, could be promoted to an embroidery position now that someone could take her place running errands. Oksoo had lost her parents at war and was introduced to my mother through her sister's orphanage. Mother gave Oksoo especially warm attention because she had no parents. Oksoo was a quick learner, and mother hoped to send her to night school. One day she pulled Oksoo aside. "Hi, Oksoo, can I see you a moment?" The girl followed obediently. "Oksoo, have you ever thought of going to school?"

"School?" the girl asked. "I couldn't even dream of it."

"Oksoo, I've been watching you closely for more than two years. You are smart, and if you study more you can do better work than embroidery. I think that, after a bit of schooling, you could really help me out. What do you think?"

"But what about school expenses?"

"Don't worry about it. I will manage it somehow." The next day mother sent her off to night school. She had to learn embroidery during the day and study at night, but she managed quite well and never idled away her time.

Thanks to Yanglim's mother, Oksoo was able to graduate night school. My mother's company had become a family.

NEW DAUGHTER AND SON

After 10 years of raising a single child, my mother had another daughter and son, one after the other, and after two years another daughter. Hwa Bong had beautiful, pale white skin like her father, and Joon's face was round and handsome. Hwa Young has big eyes and pretty face. My mother poured all her affection into raising them. God had blessed them especially, and she loved them dearly because she had waited so long for them to come. She sewed clothes for them with the material they used to make the dolls' clothes in the factory. Hwa Bong and Joon never left her side. They were quiet, mild children. In the workroom, they played on her knees or at her feet, their little hands swatting at the hem of her skirt. Mother sent them to nearby Changchung elementary school. Every morning she sent them off, following them to the end of the street and waving her hand behind them until they were out of sight.

Sometime grandmother would rebuke her, saying she was too affectionate to her children. "When they grow up, they'll be of no use." But my mother could not bear but to love her children indulgently.

DISAPPOINTMENT

"Mom, I'll be back soon," I always reassured my mother when I left the home. My mother would smile to herself proudly, and think of how much I had grown. She would think of all the years that had past, all the good and all the bad.

We moved during my second year of the elementary school because of the loudness of the marketplace nearby, and the gossip that had been spread in the area about our family. My mother had to leave her friends Mr. and Mrs. Oh, who had been like family to her. I transferred to Dae Shin Elementary School.

A few months after the move, her body began to weaken again. One night my father found her collapsed in their bedroom, sweating and gripping her stomach. Feeling her damp skin, he said, "You have a very high fever."

"I feel very sick. I have a pain in my stomach."

"Let's hurry to the hospital," said my father. Once there she was diagnosed with appendicitis.

"A little while longer and your wife might have died," the surgeon told my father. "Remember this in the future. Don't wait until the last moment for medical care."

Because of her weak constitution, my mother took two long weeks to recover, rather than the standard five days. Every day I went straight from school to my mother's hospital bed and reported to her the events of my day.

"Hwain, how did you do today in school? Did you do your studies well?" she would ask.

"Yes, Mom," I replied. "Here is my exam and work from today." I showed her my papers.

"Mom, I think I'll be the first in the class this year."

"How can this be? You've only been in school a few months."

"I don't know," I replied with a little embarrassment.

With short and fast steps, I slipped out from the hospital room.

On the last day of the school, an awards ceremony was held to honor exceptional students. My mother could not attend because of her condition, which she deeply regretted. She wasn't there to watch me receive the first place prize for my entire grade.

After two years, we moved again from our home in Pusan to Seoul. We lived in Sung Buk Dong, and I became a student in Hae Hwa Elementary School. A teacher who had worked at my old school in Pusan was working there, and we were thrilled to know at least one person in an unfamiliar place.

I was ten years old at the time. Getting to school meant navigating the enormous city, finding the one route that would lead me there. I had to take a bus, which worried my mother. Still, she felt she ought to trust me with the responsibility, and taught me how to take the bus to and from school. One day two or three months into the year, I took the wrong bus and found myself far off my map, in a place I didn't recognize. I spent the entire day searching for the right way to school, and for the bus that would take me there. As the hours passed I gave up hope of reaching school, and began searching for home. When I finally found it, and trudged into the room where my mother waited for me, I burst into tears. The next day, my mother transferred me to the nearest school, Su Song Elementary School, located just next to our house.

A year and a half after my transfer, I took the entrance exams for junior high school. I had gotten off to a shaky start in my new school in the most critical year of my studies. I did not make the highest of scores, and so I missed the chance to go to a top rank junior high school. This meant my chances of getting into a top ranked high school, and subsequently a good college, were significantly decreased. This was a crucial failure on my part, one that hit my mother hard. She stayed in bed for two months, often crying. She did not even push me to apply to a junior high school, so crushed were her hopes. Everything seemed lost. She held onto her mourning for a long time.

My father subscribed to a rather austere parenting philosophy: he mostly let us alone. Thus my mother took on all the responsibility of action and solicitation on our behalves. She would do anything to salvage my school career, and sought the advice of our relatives and sisters, entreating them to pray. At the time, many wealthy students paid money under the table to get into their schools of choice. My mother had grown so desperate that she may have taken up the chance, if she had enough money. She could not discuss the issue with her husband because he preferred to remain uninvolved. So all she had left were her hopes and her prayers.

She prayed, "God, you gave this daughter to me, and you have upheld her life and nurtured her until now. Please lead her and don't abandon her now in this time of need." When she was in labor with me she had a dream of an old white-haired man who came to her and laid his hands on her. She felt it meant that God would protect her and guide our lives. It had been a promise, and she felt in her heart that he had broken it.

After meeting with my sixth grade teacher, she decided to send me to Jung Shin Missionary School, one of the top second-rank high schools in Seoul. My mother's only interest at this point was that I go to the best school possible. It was only incidental that the school was a Christian one.

This first failure hurt my mother inexpressibly. She suffered in silence. Her husband at that time offered her no comfort. He had bought into the easy Korean patriarchy that exempt him from providing much more than financial stability to his wife and children. She, in her turn, was expected to act in certain ways, to do certain things, and to never ask for anything in return. Bearing the child and nurturing the child was the woman's responsibility and not the man's. My mother bore this responsibility with great seriousness. It was her Han. She continued to pray, asking that God resolve her grief one day in the future.

THE BEGINNING OF FAITH

As time passed after the disappointment of my final exams, my mother continued her attempts to persuade my father into action. However, he remained stubbornly uninvolved. Eventually, Mother gave up hope of boosting me to a better school by any means she could muster. Her husband's will did not support her own, and her efforts and hope ran up against the wall of his indifference.

My mother soon became convinced that it was up to her alone to support her children and their pursuits, and that she must mediate between us and our father to extract from him the funds we needed. Although Mother earned the lion's share of the family's income, she was not granted the right to make economic decisions regarding that money. She was very careful never to overpower her husband's authority, but with a little bit of pressure, she could persuade him to make the decisions she wanted.

After my academic setback, my mother generously encouraged me to pursue music. After a lot of forethought, hesitation and not a little scheming (a necessary skill for women outside of power in a patriarchal family system), she convinced her husband to purchase a piano for me. He consented, and fulfilled his role as the executive decision maker of the family.

Mother had earned a reputation in my elementary and junior high schools as a ready volunteer willing to contribute countless hours of her time to help the school. She came to appreciate the fact that the school that had accepted her daughter was Christian. She had prayed: "O God, please keep my daughter in your hands, and lead her to success in her pursuits and in her future. Amen." Now she felt that these prayers would be answered. God would nourish her faith in this school.

Prayer enabled my mother to resume life with strength, and once again she poured her energy whole-heartedly into her work as a teacher and doll maker. Her mind, however, was always with her daughter. No thoughts belonged solely to herself, no energy was expended in her own enjoyment. Having lived her childhood during the war and the reconstruction, my mother had developed a kind of urgency that informed all of her pursuits. Nothing should be wasted in efforts or pursuits that were not crucial. So she felt it right to live her life utterly for her daughter.

The days passed by in a blur. My father and mother grew apart from each other. Deeply rooted in Confucian thought, my father disapproved of Christianity. He objected to the total involvement in the church that he had witnessed in the life of his mother-in-law, who devoted all of her time and money to the church. He was afraid my mother would likewise expend herself in service to something outside of the realm of his family, and thus forbid her from attending. My mother heeded his wishes. She still believes that loud arguments between husband and wife should be avoided. God would not will that spouses fight. In their daily life together, and in their ideology and faith, my parents began to take separate paths that estranged them.

My mother did not attend any church, but she did not let her husband's aversion cripple her faith. She fostered it with prayer. Every night, though exhausted by the day's work, she poured the last of her wakeful strength into prayer. It was through these conversations with God that she kept her spiritual life vital and growing, and through her assurance that these prayers would be answered in full one day. She believed that the strife of her marriage was only an opportunity to see God's will at work in adversity. Every difficulty she faced, whether for her children or in her marriage, she accepted as a hardship of faith. To prevail over suffering was to be faithful. She prayed: "O God, let me overcome and endure these hardships in my life. May I be victorious one day. A-men."

My mother believed that patience, humility, and love were the noblest virtues, and these she upheld in her life. She taught all of these to her students, most of whom had great need for them as women who did not have the opportunity to live for themselves—to study, to spend what they earned—because their families depended financially on their incomes. So when my mother took on students, she taught them the subject matter for which her life had trained her, the values and virtues she had learned in a life of prayer.

WAE-HALMONI (MY MOTHER'S MOM)

She was very short—only four feet tall—but a clean and charming lady, always colorfully dressed. Unlike many women her age, the years had not crumpled her over. At 70 years of age she was still a strong woman at a time when not many people lived long lives. Grand parties were held to celebrate the achievement of having lived to 60 years. A 70th birthday party was a rare occasion, and thus required an even more lavish ceremony. The entire family, from in-laws to grandchildren to cousins, gathered and partook in the bowing ceremony, each wishing her a long life and good health.

My grandmother settled down with us only after short, experimental stints at the homes of her other children. No one else seemed able to endure her particularities. She was staunchly set in her ways, unwilling to yield her own preferences. She had descended from royal blood and acted the part, claiming her right to more than others would allow her. This made the task of sharing a space with her impossible for her other children. My mother was the only child of hers willing to tolerate her personality.

My mother served Grandmother each of her three meals on a little table called a bap-sang in her own room so she could eat in silence and dignity. These meals consisted of different food than those of the rest of the family, and were cooked specially and separately. They were more elaborately prepared, and included more variety and quality meats and vegetables than the rest of us were served on a regular basis. She would not eat plain white rice, so my mother cooked her healthy brown rice with beans. Often my mother prepared the country's most expensive dish for Grandmother's enjoyment—kalbi, or ribs. If she was not satisfied, she sent her dishes back to the kitchen. When the food was too salty, she would call my mother in with a cup of water, and demand that she dilute it.

The first thing my grandmother did in the morning was to comb her sparse silver hair in the short modern style of the day with a miniature comb and water. Then she donned her cleaned han-bok (Korean traditional clothes). In the winter, she would wear a vest and a half coat. She lived in a room that was heated from beneath, so the floor was always warm. She read the Bible every morning at her little table for two hours before breakfast. After breakfast, she held court in the garden where she cared for the little flowers. If it rained, she stayed in and sewed. My grandmother was not one to sit around and do nothing. As a religious women, she felt that all her time was precious and ought to be devoted to productive activity for God's glory. She was a person of action and discipline, in body and mind. She would fast, attend church anytime it was open, and tithe (more than anyone else in the family). When she worshipped in her room, we could all hear prayers resound in the halls.

Grandmother clashed with my father, perhaps because they both felt so entitled to the same things. She objected to my father's faithlessness and what she perceived to be his choice to make his wife work for their family's living. Both a wife and husband working to earn money was unusual at the time. My grandmother thought that my mother's employment depleted time that ought to be spent doing community service and volunteering with a church. She often told me, "I regret serving as the matchmaker between your mother and your father. Perhaps it would have been better had they not married." She expected my father to exhibit the reverence she felt was her due, but he too was stubborn, and refused to have an in-law order him about. While Grandmother was willing to dine with her grandchildren, she refused to eat in the presence of her son-in-law. This constant tension put a strain on my mother, who felt she owed to each her total allegiance.

My grandmother had never attended school. She learned everything in the home as she grew up. Women of her generation were rarely provided the chance to learn formally. Academic training was reserved for boys. Nevertheless, my grandmother was more intellectual, and certainly more sharp-witted than my mother. In general knowledge and in social, economic, and political issues, she was quite the master of a wide array of facts and informed opinions.

At church she was appointed a kwon-sa nim, an office higher than that of a deacon. Her responsibility included accompanying the minister to visit members of the church and advising the minister and other officials regarding church matters. Only elderly women were given this title and responsibility in recognition of their wisdom.

Grandmother's prayers at the church were unmatched by any other member. The spiritual depth and content of her prayers strengthened the community of believers around her. She took pride in her faith. Always aware of her high position in the church, she conducted herself with special care so that others could emulate her.

Ultimately, my mother had a hard time living with her mother. The demands she imposed were far beyond her Confucian entitlements. It was more difficult than living with her own mother-in-law! But my mother remained obedient and dutiful. She was a good daughter to her mother.

MOTHER STRENGTHENED ME

Whenever my classes finished for the day, I would walk out onto the second floor patio where I could see the playground below and the school gate beyond it. Students would begin to trickle out into the sunlight and, gathered in pockets all around me, they would rest and chat and make plans for the rest of the day. In the playground, girls walked arm in arm, jumped rope, and played hop-scotch. I'd watch them quietly and wonder what I was doing here, why I had ended up in this place. I would think of what my mother had wanted for me, of her failing efforts to find a top-rank school for me to attend instead of this one. I wondered if I had become a failure. I was young and didn't yet know who I was, who I'd become. I had thought I'd known the path that would take me to success, but it seemed I'd taken a wrong turn.

I don't know how many days I repeated this routine. I adjusted to my new environment, but I never warmed to it. I still felt that I didn't belong there.

"Hwain," my mother called one day. "How are you doing in school these days?"

"It's all right, Mom." I answered dully.

"Did you make many friends yet?"

"No." I replied with resignation.

"Do you know," my mother kept after me, "that Korean proverb: 'Failure is the mother of success'? Try hard and then become a bigger person for it. Look at me. Have hope. If you have hope, you will achieve what you want in the future. If you pray hard, you will get an answer. I believe God will listen to you." My mother's words struck my heart. My spirit awoke like a rabbit before a hunter's gun. In all my indulgent misery I had removed myself from life as though I were dreaming. I had not been living, not making choices, not acting. I decided I must wake up and commit myself to the path to which God had led me. I would work harder at school and not waste my time regretting and longing for other things.

The next morning, I woke with a new attitude. How anxious I was to go to school! I proudly donned my white collared shirt and navy uniform, and in the street I joined the line of others wending their way to school. I passed the marshals with their sashes, stationed at checkpoints to check hair and skirt lengths and the cleanliness of our uniforms and shoes. By the time I entered the classroom the first bell had rung. We each picked up our cushion and Bible, and in a line of navy colored bodies marched to the auditorium for the morning worship which commenced the school day.

As my mother had told me, hope opens life so that we can see the possibility in it for what we desire. She had said, "Because I have hope, I have been able to live." I knew that I had become her hope—all the happiness and success I might achieve. With new hope, I worshipped with the others and my heart was sustained.

As my day continued, I was constantly reminded of my mother's love for me. Each day at lunch, students opened their boxes to uniform lumps of rice and vegetables mixed carelessly together, or a bowl of rice with a friend egg on top, which made a messy meal. But my lunch box was always clean and well-ordered, each dish separately packed. My mother took such special care to arrange my meals, and each day prepared a different kind of meat for me. It made me proud to have a mother who tried so hard to make my day the best it could be.

Our lunch hour was long, and I usually finished eating with plenty of time to spare. Afterwards, I would go up to the attic above the auditorium where there was a small dark prayer room. There were always four or five others there, kneeling on the ground, mumbling softly. My first visit, I hesitated at the doorway, looking in at the others. No one looked up, so I slipped quietly in and kneeled down among the low bodies. I kept my face close to the floor so that no one would have the chance to recognize me. Every day I came to this room to meditate and to pray: O God you have told me that if I have hope, I have possibility. Why did you deny my mother's hope that I attend a good school? I know you have given each of us a certain purpose for our lives. What is your purpose on me?

I spent my middle school lunch hours in prayer, crying to God for direction and purpose. Afterwards, I wiped my wet eyes, blew my nose, and joined the rest of my classmates for afternoon classes. Prayer gave me hope and expectation. I awaited an answer.

A NEW FRIEND

My mother's younger sister had become a successful business women and held a prominent place in her community. Her husband had been the Finance Minister of Korea before the division. The story of his capture had touched the hearts of many, and his wife became close friends with the President and the members of Congress and the cabinet. On New Year's Day she and her children, wearing beautiful han boks(Traditional Korean dress), visited the President's home.

My mother was proud of her sister and felt a deep love for her nephew and niece, whose father had been taken from them. They were beautiful children, strikingly so. She helped them in any way they needed. Although Confucian custom dictated that a younger sister treat her elder siblings with deference, my mother was the one to honor her sister. In fact, my aunt treated Mother more like a hired servant than an elder sister. Still, my mother had only unconditional love for her sister.

My cousins lived luxuriously. Their mother's wealth and status secured for them the best tutors and tuitions to top schools. My mother regretted that she could not send me to piano school or dance classes, which my cousins were able to afford. Sometimes I tagged along with my cousins to their daily activities and envied their luck. My mother often asked me if I would like to take the same classes, but I knew there was no way we could afford them. The more significant hurdle, however, was perhaps my father's tightfistedness. He deemed these activities luxuries and not necessities in the country's difficult economic times.

One day, returning home from school, I had news from my mother—a chance to take dancing classes. I asked her, "Mom, can I take dancing lessons as part of the school's extra-curricular program?"

She seemed shocked at the opportunity. I continued, "Today, our dancing class teacher, Miss Lee, told me that she wanted to see me after class, so I stayed after all the other kids left. Then she told me that there are after-school classes at the school, and she asked me to join the dance group. I told her I'd ask you."

My mother had been troubled by what she felt I was missing out on. She wanted my life to be as rich and full as those of my cousins who wanted for nothing. She grew excited.

"What will you do if you join this dance group?" she asked me.

"It means that after school is over, I go to the dance studio for a couple of hours every day for practice. Once a year there's a performance recital."

"Do we have to pay?" she asked warily.

"No, it's free!"

My mother was thrilled to hear this, because it meant that her husband could not object.

My dance teacher, Ms. Lee, was a thin woman with a sharp nose. She wore leotards and her hair styled short like a ballerina. She had a look austerity because of her angular dancer's physique, but I remember her as a woman with an overflowing heart. She was unmarried, but became a maternal figure to all of students, caring and nurturing us through the vicissitudes of adolescent life.

She and my mother became friends, and began to call each other "sister." She would tell my mother, "Don't worry about Hwain. As long as I'm in the school with her, I will take care and watch over her." My mother was relieved to have such a warm presence in her life and my own. They would meet to discuss my progress and to talk about their own lives, their struggles. Together, they dealt with problems only women have, pooling their resources to determine the best course of action. They fortified one another, and helped each other to endure. This friendship was a source of relief to my mother during unstable times.

The dance recital was always held in the fall. My mother was so proud to see me alongside the other dancers. She even helped out back stage with the preparations for the performance. Her friend, too, flitted here and there tightening the bows on our costumes, touching up our make-up, and conducting warm-up exercises. My mother was glad to help her friend, and to see that her friend cared for me as well.

PRESIDENT SEUNGMAN RHEE

One day at school, during lunch hour, an announcement came on the loudspeakers that everyone should convene outside on the school grounds. The president was coming into town, and we were to salute him as he drove past. School officials gave each of us a Korean flag and led us single-file to one of Seoul's major streets, Chong-Ro Sa Ga. Businessmen and residents who had already heard the news were already in place on the sidewalk. We students were right at the curb. Police officers mounted on horses kept the crowds in line as the president's entourage neared. The streets were cleared of vehicles, and the normally bustling street eerily emptied of traffic. All the electric streetcars, trucks, and bicycles had been relocated somewhere out of sight.

Finally, the sirens of the first motorcycles sounded nearby, announcing the approach of the president. Black limousines with smoky glass windows passed, holding unseen passengers. Then the black convertible limousine bearing the president rolled through, and he waved to us. He had white hair like a grandfather, and seemed dignified and benevolent, beaming his warm smile at us.

We spent most of the rest of the day lingering in the street in his wake before returning to school and sitting through the rest of our classes. During the final class of the day, our teacher announced that each school in the nation was having its students write essays to commemorate the president's birthday. We got out our notebooks and began to compose our remembrance of the day.

Until that day, I had only ever seen the president on television, in the newspaper, or in a picture my aunt had on her wall of the man standing with my cousins. But today I'd seen him up close—he had passed just in front of me. I felt very close to him, almost as though he was a member of my own family. I entitled my composition "President Grandfather" and wrote addressing him as I would my own grandfather. My composition wasn't long—just a few paragraphs. After a few days, it was announced that my essay had been selected to receive first prize out of all the other middle school students in Korea.

I was incredibly surprised. It was unbelievable. My mother had already been notified by the school before I arrived home that day. When I met her after school, she congratulated me warmly. "Hwain, you were chosen for your writing."

Seeing my mother filled with joy made me proud. Only, I wondered what all the fuss was. I had just written down what I'd been feeling. My mother, however, was thrilled that her daughter was playing piano, dancing, and now, writing at the level of celebrity. She was bursting with pride and gratitude that her prayers were being granted. She redoubled her efforts on my behalf. This success seemed to cancel out the failures that had come before. I could tell that we had turned a corner, and a new phase of our lives was beginning.

DILEMMA

"Mom, Hyun-Sup wants to enter a high ranking high school, and she told me she wants me to go with her. Do you think that I can?"

Hyun-Sup was a strongly gifted student, and I wanted to follow her lead.

Mom listened quietly to my entire story, and when I was finished only said, "Daughter, do what you want to do." My mother did not want to give me a decision. She wanted me to make it for myself and choose the course I wanted.

I told her eagerly what I perhaps had already resolved upon. "Mom, I'll try to make it a good move, and I'll study very hard."

So I began at once to study with Hyun-Sup in order to do well on the entrance exams, now only a year away. While I danced after school, Hyun-Sup also practiced her piano. Afterward we met in the school's library and kept our noses in our books until it closed at 9:00 at night. We were not alone there. Many fellow students were also getting ready for these all-important exams.

When I got home, I studied in my room alone, even when the electricity went out. My mother gave me candles to study by in the dark. She gave me two candles, already lit. "Hwain, one is not enough. One candle is too dim, so you need at least two." With two candles perched above my notes and books, I studied through the night, resolving only to sleep when the candles disappeared to nubs and pools of wax.

"Hwain! Are you not sleepy? Here's some American coffee to help keep you awake. Are you hungry? Do you want something to eat?" Even in the dead of night, my mother stayed awake with me. She was tirelessly attentive, listening through the walls for the rustle of my pages turning. She was over 40 years old, but unlike other women, she did not exercise the luxury of having a mid-life crisis. She continued to busy herself with the lives and well-being of others, and with me in particular.

The anticipation and joy of transferring to a new school was mitigated in only one respect: it meant saying goodbye to Ms. Lee, who had become so important to me and my mother. I knew she would be devastated to lose me as a student and quite possibly my mother as a friend. I found myself avoiding her in the halls, oppressed by a sense of guilt. Ms. Lee had helped me to develop an identity; she had been a source of strength. I had been missing rehearsals for our upcoming recital, and couldn't bring myself to tell her that my secret studying sessions were the cause. Jung Shin had its own high school, which middle school students were encouraged to attend, so last year middle school students were solicited by teachers and administrators. If the school lost its best students, the school's statistic of college-bound high school seniors would suffer.

My mother finally decided to tell Ms. Lee about my decision. They met at a local tea house, and my mother tentatively began, "Teacher Lee, don't be hurt. Hwain is only thinking of her future."

Ms. Lee immediately caught on. "I had a feeling Hwain wanted to transfer, but how can it possibly be? No, she cannot leave the school. Do you know how much I love her? Transferring schools is no guarantee that Hwain will enter a good college. Please reconsider." Her eyes were brimming with tears. She spoke of other students who had transferred but had ended up failing at the high school level after facing increased academic demands. Her arguments weakened my mother's confidence in my ability to choose my future's course. Perhaps there were difficulties I couldn't foresee on my own. She wondered if we were risking another failure.

After that meeting, I could not avoid Ms. Lee, who barraged me with example after example of the myriad possibilities of failure which awaited me. She reminded me constantly of my excellent progress in dancing under her tutelage over the past three years. We parted many times in silent anger. She refused to give me her blessing and would not write a recommendation letter for me.

My closest friend Hyun-Sup continued without me, and I stopped my studying. I graduated from the Jung Shin High School. I lost track of my friend for years until we met in America at Columbia University

SISTERHOOD

More than fifty people altogether lived under our roof—artisans, students and workers in my mother's employ, and my mother, father, two sisters, brother, and me. My mother was the matriarch of the household, its chief administrative officer. Above her in the household hierarchy was only Halmoni (grandmother), to whom my mother was an exemplary and obedient daughter. She was also a good wife to her husband, a wise mother to her children, and a kind, sympathetic teacher to her embroidery students. Usually women in their forties strayed from the domesticity that by then had become a clear impediment to their own personal fulfillment. Being a mother and wife required endless, often excruciating self-sacrifice and left little for a woman to have for herself. But any betrayal of her maternity or responsibility was not an option for my mother. Instead, she continued to live for others, and to shape herself according to her relationships. She was giving yet strong, flexible yet aware of her boundaries. Traditionally, women were on the margins of power in a home dominated by a man. My mother's life, however, was the central pillar of our huge household. She supported everyone. She bore all the weight. Her dignity would not allow anyone to push her around.

My mother never lost a sense of her own importance in the relationship she maintained with her younger sister, the world traveler and famous political figure. She remained the ever dutiful elder sister, reserving and then exercising for herself the duties and rights that were her due. Over the years, my mother's sister became more and more masculine in that she rejected the traditional occupations to which women were expected to devote themselves. She was a businesswoman, a traveler, and a public figure who did not spend all of her time in the home. Perhaps because she had taken on the role society consigned to men, she felt entitled to its rights as well. She found in my mother a woman on which she could pour her frustrations whenever business was bad, or her fortunes took a regretful turn. Such scourges my mother took in stride, even though it strained their relationship. My mother's patience and love allowed their relationship to remain sound.

"A TUTOR MALSOON AND COLLEGE"

A great hope for my mother was that I go to a good college. My mother had regretted that her life's circumstances had not allowed her to attend, and she was eager to secure for me the opportunity she had never had. So my mother did whatever she could to help boost my studies so I could do well on the entrance exams and earn a spot at one of the nation's most prestigious schools. She herself hadn't the time or the learning to help me with my high school studies, so she arranged for a private tutor to prepare me.

The tutor she found was a young woman who attended Seoul National University, one of the best schools in Korea, and studied physics. My mother welcomed her into our house and paid her college tuition. She asked Malsoon to treat me like her own sister. Malsoon promised to do her best.

Teacher Malsoon, only four feet tall, encouraged me in all of my studies and activities. She helped me especially in math and physics, and under her tutelage I got the first place score in Physics. Teacher Malsoon, however, objected to my involvement in music and dance, which were also dear to my mother as a privilege she had never had. She urged my mother to stop the lessons because they consumed so much crucial time, so my mother finally relented and I quit piano.

As college exam time drew near, the three of us had to decide what department I should apply to. My mother wanted me to be a doctor who could cure illnesses and help those in need, but she feared a repeat of my failure to perform on the middle school entrance exams. We finally decided on educational psychology. All the members of my family and the employees who lived with us shared a moment of complete joy when my name was announced on the radio among the list of others who had passed the exam. My mother cried with delight. I was so nervous before the announcement that I'd spent the entire day roaming the streets. I only heard the news when I wandered back that night. Malsoon lived with us even after I entered college and continued to counsel me regarding my future.

V.

Social Activities

MOTHER'S SOCIAL ACTIVITIES

MY MOTHER NURTURED MANY students and housed them with us. My aunt was a lecturer of embroidery at YWCA and travelled to foreign countries to teach, and when the job tired her out, she suggested my mother as her substitute. At the Seoul YWCA in Myung Dong, my mother had her first taste of the world outside her home. This removal from the hubbub of the house and all her responsibilities there, even for only a few hours a week, gave her immense relief. She made an event of her outings there.

She took great pleasure in my entrance into college, and felt all the pressure of her motherhood ease as she began to find her own pursuits. Her business responsibilities she conferred upon her students, and rearranged her life to make time for the things she wanted to do. She often went out for luncheon meetings with her high school friends and started taking a cooking class. But she still thought of me constantly, and used her cooking class to equip her to teach me how to be a good housewife. She practiced the day's learning by preparing the same meal she had learned to cook in class for our dinner. She even taught me how to use various, particular utensils, even though I didn't pay much attention to that. Her cooking was as beautifully prepared as her embroidery, and we often hesitated to destroy it by eating it.

MOTHER AS A GRADUATE STUDENT

Springtime at Ewha was beautiful. The gate spread along the street that led to the Shin Chon Rotary, and beyond them were pear trees in bloom all over campus. The flowers, our school symbol, were soft and dark pink and nodded in the breezes over our heads, over the paths and the grass. Students would lounge in the sun on the stairs of the main auditorium, waiting for their next classes. Up these stairs we clattered in our high heels for worship at the chapel.

I attended the Morning Prayer meeting which started at 6 o'clock AM at the Ewha garden. There, I could see the school president Ok Kil Kim seated a short distance away. Only about seven or eight students attended in a student body of ten thousand. I enjoyed observing the president who seemed to hold herself with such dignity and exuded a kind of brightness of spirit. Her conversation was full of wit and her prayers were short but clear.

One day she kindly called my name and asked about my mother. "Hwain how is your mother? Is she busy as usual? How is her YWCA work?"

"She is fine."

"We recently opened graduate school for mothers. How about asking your mother to take a class? It would be a good opportunity for her."

Her suggestion filled me with joy. I thought it'd be wonderful to study with my mother and share with her the campus I'd come to love. I promised the president I'd give my mother the application sheet. The news thrilled my mother. The new graduate school provided a two-year reeducation program for mothers and was not require undergraduate schooling. I persuaded her that this was her opportunity to study like she had wanted when she was younger. With my father's permission, she began to attend classes twice a week.

I accompanied her to her classroom for the first couple of classes until she was settled. My class was on the other side of campus, so we parted at the bus stop, always waving goodbye.

Mother finished the school when I advanced to my junior year. She was a model student in the school and was known to the president as Hwain's mother.

SISTER JIN YONG AND MOTHER

It was not by chance that I chose educational psychology as my undergraduate major. I wanted to satisfy mother's hopes for me. She had wanted me to learn about the deeper meanings of life, and to be a doctor.

In my classes I met Jin Yong, 3 years my senior. Jin Yong also grew close to my mother. She visited our house often and she took good care of me at school, for which my mother was very grateful. Jin Yong was a few years behind in her studies, perhaps because of problems in her family.

Jin Yong asked my mother to let me be a member of YWCA. She got permission from my mother that I could participate in many YWCA programs to which she always escorted me. My mother appreciated that Jin Yong helped me to become involved in activities that served the community. She herself enjoyed her lectureship with the YWCA, so she eagerly encouraged my own participation. Jin Yong became my closest friend and sister and has always guided me since, becoming like a part of my family.

WORLD CHRISTIAN STUDENT CONFERENCE

In 1967, I was unexpectedly elected a chairman of the Korean National Student YWCA. A young man named Bill was elected a chairman of the board of directors of the National Student YMCA Confederation. I congratulated him as a chairwoman of the counterpart. In the next year, we were both nominated as delegates to the 1968 World Student Conference in Helsinki, Finland.

I was planning to perform a Kayageum Solo. I had been studying Korean traditional music as a hobby and the teachers and friends asked me to perform at the conference. Many elders, friends and teachers encouraged me and the concert was very successful, garnering an unexpectedly big audience. Bill was there among my enthusiastic supporters.

In the beginning of December, the YWCA planned a student celebration for Christmas and we did our best to prepare. Many stores where the students shopped donated gifts. All the members worked hard, and I always felt sorry that much of the praise was given to the leaders and not the individuals who had put in so much time and effort.

The thing I remember best about the night was when Bill gave me a gift. It was shoes he had won as a third place prize in Bingo. He had come with a date, and I remember feeling guilty that I had received a gift from him. At the end of the night he escorted me home.

After that, Bill and I met each other often at the YM-YW executive meetings. We had many discussions during the Christian Professor's meetings, student representative meetings, and joint staff meetings. The work we did in the student YWCA confederation included writing reports about the programs we held, analyzing issues, and suggesting new directions for the programs of YWCA. The big programs included the national seasonal conference held jointly between the YMCA and the YWCA. The winter conference of the year was held at Jensen Hall from morning until night.

Bill and I were both living in Seoul and prepared for the World Conference together. He was a senior in medical school and two years older than me, so I felt I could learn from him. We studied the country of Finland, famous for its deep forests and the white nights of its summers, where the conference would be held. We also learned that it was very difficult to get a visa to travel there because it was a neutralized country. We studied the main theological lines of thought of the time. We found the lectures of Prof. Young Hak Hyun and of Rev. Kye Joon Lee the most valuable and interesting. We studied sometimes in our living room and sometimes in our professor's study. Together we relished the emergence of new trends in theology that helped to reshape our attitudes.

It soon became the season of cherry blossoms. Buds bloomed all around the Ewha campus. The air became hot and damp in anticipation of the May Day festival. The thing I looked forward to most was the dance party held in the main ground. The senior class was given the most favors. Most students came with their fiancés or boyfriends. I attended with Bill.

One day in June, a few days before our departure to Finland, we were studying at my house. I was enjoying learning from him, but my position in the organization made me cautious. That night, he proposed to me. I was faced with a big choice. I had received some requests from boys my age for dates and had humbly refused them, but this was very different. We were going to travel together and I liked him so much. I asked him to give me time to think about my answer.

We departed for Finland. I was very excited to ride an airplane for the first time. I remember that I prayed to thank God so many time while were in the air. I thanked him for giving me a position in the organization, something I had not deserved.

MARRIAGE OF A DAUGHTER

During our preparations for the world student conference, Bill often came to our house. My mother always welcomed him and played the hostess. She paid no attention at first to his background or even his personality. She only treated him as she did the other students who visited her daughter. While we worked she served us tea and fruit. Even when she sensed our growing closeness, she expressed no concern, only told me: "It's up to you." She did not think of whether he was good enough, but whether we ourselves made a good impression. She worried whether her daughter behaved well or whether our household was worse than others. She instructed me never to disgrace the honor of our household.

It was only when we began to discuss the schedule and plan for our engagement that she needed assurance that the man I would marry was a good one who would give me the best life. She felt at ease when she heard that her future son-in-law was a grandson of the Dr. Yong Sul Lee, an elder of Severance Medical School, very famous at the time. Her future son-in-law descended from a faithful man, a man of knowledge.

Mother thanked God that her beloved daughter found a man she wanted to marry. She only regretted not preparing better for the inevitable separation. Mother shed tears every night at the thought of letting go of the companion who had sustained her and whom she had sustained for so much of her life. Long prayers she poured out for her daughter's future. When the time of the wedding approached, she devoted herself to its preparations. She prepared with her own hands gifts to be given the esteemed house of my father-in-law.

My mother kept all the traditional customs that the bride's house should keep. She said that the bride and bridegroom should stay the first night in the bride's home and she prepared the delicious menu us. Afterwards, I moved to Bill's house in Shin Chon and we began our married life there. One elder sister-in-law and two younger in-laws lived with us. All the household goods that mother had prepared for us without my knowing were sent to the Shin Chon house. As I spread them out and looked over the Noridake dish sets and silver spoon sets my mother had arranged so carefully with her little fingers, I regretted my thoughtlessness in having left so suddenly. I had been so excited to begin anew, I had forgotten to thank her, to make more of our separation.

VI.

To the USA

GOING ON A JOURNEY

ONE CUSTOM WIDELY PRACTICED in Korea is to throw a big celebration for a baby's first birthday. Even though we were moving to the United States in only five days, we decided to throw little John a big party to commemorate his first year of life. We knew this might be the last time the entire family could convene together in Korea, so we urged all our relatives to attend and to bid us goodbye. I was eight months pregnant with my second child at the time, but, the excitement of the event swept me up and put me work.

When the big day finally arrived, our house filled and brimmed over with uncles, aunts, grandmothers, grandfathers, and cousins, some I had not even met before. We made sure to have plenty of food to fill everyone up. It was a hot summer day. The rose bushes were burning their colors under the sun—yellow, red, and pink against the neatly clipped green lawn. While John splashed around in the small swimming pool under the shade of the maple tree, I prepared all the well-known favorites of Korean cuisine, delicacies the day demanded.

We had already given away all our possessions in preparation for the big move that was to be a real beginning. Our car, the pool, all of John's toys, our dishes, pots, pans, and china we all divvied up amongst our love ones who would stay behind. Everything we wanted to keep we had to ship the long way to our new home in the states.

Boarding the plane was a challenge with a baby and his trappings in tow, and with my own swollen belly getting in the way. I had to cling to hope and to the thrill of this new journey, and to leave behind the sorrow of having to part. We said our goodbyes and made our promises to reunite soon. Then we set ourselves to the path ahead.

It was a marvel how many bodies could be crammed into that airplane. Some were undoubtedly emigrating just as we were; others were perhaps going on business trips or vacations. We were just barely able to weave our way through to our seats, which were fortunately in the front of the plane with the other families with small children. During the long plane ride, I broke out into cold sweats, just praying, pleading that John would be able to sleep and that he wouldn't burst into sobs that would disturb the others. Then there was the fact that I was eight months pregnant. I remember taking comfort in the presence of my husband Bill sitting beside me, probably churning the many responsibilities, details, and fears over silently in his mind. I was relieved that I had someone to share it all with.

Kennedy Airport, in my memory, was a dark place. All I remember was that we were greeted by some relatives who had come to meet us. Later that night we arrived at their house. But very early the next morning Bill had to take a train to the hospital where he worked.

Due to various complications in obtaining our passports and visas we were delayed one month in arriving in the United States. Naturally the first thing Bill wanted to do upon arriving was to find out whether his position at the hospital was still being held for him.

At the time I could not fathom how Bill could just pick up and go into a city completely foreign to him, and find his way by train and taxi, a trip that took three hours in total, to the hospital. When he returned late that night, he announced that the position was still his, and that he had secured us a three-bedroom apartment.

The very next day we moved into the apartment that was to be our home for our first year in the United States. We traversed the streets of Brooklyn, streets I had never seen before but about which I had heard plenty. Our apartment was on the third floor of a four-story building. The apartment was reserved for hospital staff and was bare except for a few measly furnishings. With its high ceilings and enormous window in the living room, the place looked naked. Empty space and not human warmth seemed to claim the place. At night when we switched on the lights, we felt that everyone in the streets below and in the buildings adjacent could see into our lives. But we were ultimately too exhausted to do anything but rest. Stowing our baggage in a corner, we put John on bed and settled down to sleep. Breathing a big sigh of relief, we said to each other, "Whew, we're finally home!" and so spent our first night in our new nest, filled with expectations for the days ahead.

BROOKLYN THROUGH A WINDOW

The newness of our surroundings catapulted us into unremitting heights of stress and anxiety. In the aftermath of our departure from Korea, I was shocked and perhaps proud of how eager we had been to throw ourselves into this new environment. Our fears had not been as great as our desire to begin anew. Bill's life as an intern meant starting at the hospital at eight each morning and working on-call through the night every three days. On these days he'd return home at five in the morning and tumble immediately into bed. In the evening when he woke, he took the dirty laundry and the baby's diapers to the Laundromat across the street. With the washers running, he'd run over to the A&P a few blocks away and do our grocery shopping before the store closed at six.

As for me, I had my hands full with John. Less than a month after our arrival, I gave birth to our second son Charles. With two infants in need of constant care, I no longer saw the light of day outside our apartment. A kind of fear had grown in me since we'd arrived, especially after having heard so many stories about how unsafe Brooklyn was. Citing the excuse that I knew no English, I avoided leaving our little safe haven in the city.

When Bill left and the door shut with a bang I locked it immediately. At the center of the door at eye level, there was a peephole about the size of my pinky through which I could verify who was at the door when the bell rang or someone knocked. My one favorite features of our new home was the enormous living room window through which I could look out into the street facing our apartment. Strangers and cars passed endlessly by. That first night at the apartment the gaping window had seemed like a breach in our new found safety. I had felt that it would give away our secrets, expose us to unwelcome eyes. But it soon became my only friend, my only connection to the world outside. I longed for contact and involvement in that scene of bustling life outside, but was too afraid to achieve it.

As the days wore on and Bill continued his arduous internship, he struggled to adjust to the grueling hours. I watched him change into man twisted and wrenched by stress. He seemed more to me like a machine going about his routine than a responsive, vibrant human being. His internship was to last one year, after which he would have to apply for a residency position. He had just become the father of two young boys, but he was conscious only of his upcoming medical exam in September. Perhaps the only way for him to survive the strain was to become more mechanical.

These were long and exhausting days that allowed me little time of my own, but I resolved never to pity myself or complain about my hardship. I had prepared and coached myself mentally and accept whatever difficulties came. I remember how absolutely determined I was to do all that I could to be a good mother to my children and to take care of myself for Bill's sake. I knew he would be put to the test with this new job, and that it would occupy him entirely, so I resolved not to expect anything from him.

So as to give Bill peace when he was studying in his room, I would take the children with me to a small room farthest from his. There I would placate every whim and wish of the children so that Bill could study in quiet. I played endlessly with them whatever games they wanted. I'd sit and tickle them or give them rides on my back. Whenever my energy was sapped, I'd urge them to look out the window at what lay outside. The window took up my charge nobly, and played before their eyes a million colors and faces and shapes and objects moving and changing. These entertained the children and gave me a chance to find my breath.

As time passed and I grew more accustomed to our hectic pace of life, I began to devise more creative ways of caring for my two small children. Both of them needed constant attention, so when I fed one, the other cried and waited. But I found that if I laid both down and secured little Charles with blankets and pillows, I could feed both simultaneously by holding one bottle to their lips with each hand. Other times I would roll John in a stroller with my foot to assuage him while feeding Charles in my arms. I came up with various little tricks to get me through all the myriad tasks of caring for children. The one thing I could not figure out was what to do when both babies required a diaper change at the same time. I always wondered whether they were in some kind of conspiracy against me. My attention had to go to the one who cried the hardest, and the less demanding one waited out his turn.

When I finally tucked both children into their beds and made sure they were asleep, I would often come to my window. At times I would hear the siren of an ambulance and look out the window, wondering if it were traveling to Bill's hospital, and who it carried in tow. Each day I looked out into the street from my darkened room, waiting for Bill's homecoming so that I could meet him at the door. I would sometimes be reminded of the window that Anne Frank spoke of in her diary. I would look out my window and pass the night thinking about the people I saw and the various stories their lives might tell.

LETTERS FROM THE UNITED STATES

After my mother sent me off, she cried every night. Her sense of loss was so great that she dreamed of me whenever she slept. The only contact between us that could sustain her was the letters we sent to one another. Each day she trekked to the mail box to see if a letter had arrived. Only from these morsels could she have any idea of what her daughter's life was like in the United States. These letters described moments in my life—touchdown at the airport, the visit to our cousins' home in Long Island, Bill's commute to the city by train, and the move to our apartment in Brooklyn. I tried to describe in vivid detail all the sensations and feelings that welled up in me during my trip so that I could transmit a little piece of myself back to my mother.

These letters relieved my mother, and let her feel some joy for me. Frequent calls were prohibitively expensive, but on the rare occasions her daughter's voice trickled through the line, she felt all her concerns appeased, if only for a little while. In between calls, letters, and reports, Mother was hostage to her own imagination about what was happening to her daughter on the other side of the world; she had countless fears, had heard hundreds of stories. It was only when she heard back that the jumble of her mind's misgivings resolved on clear, comforting images of the Brooklyn apartment and of the events of our lives.

Letter followed letter. Each one was full of good news, each a picture of a new life, and each one reinforcing her resolve to immigrate to the United States. In the depths of her heart, she wanted to go. Indeed, children often left first in order to prepare a place for the rest of the family, who would arrive later. In reply, my mother wrote: "Extend to me an invitation to come and live with you in the United States. Let me help you with your new son. Let me be a part of your life again." After eight months of being apart from her daughter, Mother left her three children and husband and boarded a plane for New York.

EIGHT MONTHS' SEPARATION

Eight months we were apart, but it felt to my mother like eight long years of separation. We loved and had come to depend on each other so deeply that it was impossible to live so far from each other any longer. My mother resolved to move to the United States to be with me.

After my marriage, my mother's business had begun to shrink. She busied herself with its affairs without much help from my father. She had three children left to take care of, and felt she could not yet retire if she wanted to secure the best financial future for them. She thought of me in America, and wished I were with her to counsel and support her.

She and my father discussed her trip for many weeks before she decided to leave. They determined that in her absence the family would move to our Myung Il Dong house, where a woman who worked for us (ajooma) was living. It was painful for my mother to leave her three children behind. Hwa Bong was in high school, Joon was in middle school, and Hwa Young was in primary school. Mother was uncertain about her future and suffered from the guilt of her impending departure. She wondered whether she was evading her responsibility to the rest of their children, each still quite young. "Hwa Bong, you should behave as the eldest daughter while I am away."

"I know mother. You go there and make all the preparations to bring the rest of us soon."

Hearing Hwa Bong's response, my mother cried. "Listen to your father and ajoomma, and take good care of Joon and Hwa Young. You are big enough to do that." Mother knew that Hwa Bong was a little cool and tended to be neat; she wanted her daughter to be softer towards her younger siblings. Joon was a calm child, and Mother hoped that he would stir up no problems. Hwa Young was a little girl and mother entrusted her to the care of the ajooma.

At last mother and the rest of the family moved to the Myung Il dong house. The date of mother's departure drew near. Mother entreated ajoomma to take good care of her husband and children.

She promised to invite the family to America soon, although she was not certain about the future. Her heart was almost broken. She felt as though she were discarding her own children and husband.

She prayed: "God, would is this the right thing to do? Only you understand my mind. Please hold me and guide my future, Amen."

THE BEGINNING OF THE IMMIGRANT LIFE

All Mother had heard of America had come from the mouths of others or from books. Kennedy Airport with its vast spaces and clean lines impressed her, and seemed infinitely grander than the airport in Seoul. She arrived at our Brooklyn apartment at midnight, bearing with her piles of packages and bags full of necessities for the babies, and food from Korea that we had missed. The apartment had no elevator, so my mother and I lugged all of our acquired possessions up the stairs. She brought a quilt for the babies, dried squid, laver, dried sea weed, a set of silver spoons, and enough underwear to last me and my husband five years.

She started her new life that first day of her arrival. While my husband studied for his test, she occupied the children. She chased John who was one and half years and was beginning to walk. She fed Charles, only six months old. Worried that their crying would disturb their slumbering father, my mother was on alert for any peep the babies made; when she heard them she scurried to their side and assuaged them before they could wake him. She was worrying that the children might awaken her son-in-law who fell asleep after overnight work. Much of the housework she took into her charge; she even bought material for curtains and made them with her own hands for our big living room window.

Before my mother came, I could hardly ever leave the house with the children, because I was afraid I wouldn't be able to control them. I couldn't shop with them because I couldn't carry them both and the groceries up to the fourth floor. But with my mother there to support me, I could take them out into the sunshine, and stroll them to the discount store ten blocks away, where we bought fabric for less than fifty cents a yard. My mother's presence seemed to open up all the strictures that had made life in Brooklyn such a strain. She helped me with the children and cooked us delicious food even on our budget. She bathed the children and put them to bed before my husband arrived home so that he could eat in peace. She let me rest and allowed for my husband to concentrate fully on his tests.

At first I worried that she was doing too much, but I soon realized that it was her only desire to help us. My husband advised me not to let her do my own work for me. I did my best to balance the workload between us. She quickly became a crucial member of our little family unite. Perhaps it was easier on her with us because she had less people to serve than she did in Korea. She took pleasure in her work, and we were grateful to be together again.

THE HARDSHIPS AND THE PLEASURES

My mother's days in America were busy. All day she cared for me and my children. Often she thought of the family back in Korea. She trusted ajooma with them, but she was sorry to have left her children at such crucial moments in their lives. Hwa Bong and Joon were growing to maturity and would miss her guidance. She could not be there for them as she had been for me. But Mother comforted herself with the thought that her move to America was the best thing for the family's future. She shed tears often at night and prayed, "God, you understand the mind of this little one. Forgive me if I did anything wrong. Please lead me to the right way. I will bear all these sufferings if it will bring peace to my family. If this isn't the right way, then please let our family join together again." Even though her daughter's attentive care comforted her, it was not easy for Mother to live with her son-in-law. She tried not to intrude on the time that he and I shared, nor did she insist that she get her way in ever matter. She only thanked God for allowing her to be with her daughter, and continued to pray.

TO NEW JERSEY

Three months passed after my mother's arrival, Bill passed his test and received acceptance letters from several hospitals for the position of resident. Wayne General Hospital in Detroit and New Jersey University Hospital drew my husband's interest most as the best options for pursuing a career track in cardiology. After visiting the two hospitals, he chose the New Jersey University Hospital, where he felt it would be easier for him to take a teaching position, and where he would have more opportunities to practice.

We had heard that Newark was not a safe place to live with children, so after 2 months searching for an apartment near the New Jersey University Hospital, we found a cozy two bedroom in Belleville that seemed to fit our needs. Rent was $230 a month. It was 20 minutes from the hospital in Newark.

A new life began again. We enjoyed all the space we had in New Jersey. We had forgotten how much pleasure the earth could give us, and what sunlight looked like every day when it fell on grass and not concrete. We had a small backyard where the children could play. My mother enjoyed bushing the stroller around town, and making clothes for the boys with her own hands. To ease her process, I bought her a sewing machine in installments. It was what she needed most.

AMERICAN GRANDMOTHER

Mother gradually got accustomed to life in America, and to life with my new little family. The American life seemed to her full of luxury. At the grocery store, so many different kinds of food glittered under the lights, and were cheaper than those in Korea. There was so much she had never seen before, so many new household items to choose from. She made American style kimchi with cabbages or cucumbers, and delicious soy bean paste soup with fresh vegetables.

We often made trips to the Korean grocery store in Manhattan and bought our Korean necessities such as thick soy bean paste mixed with red peppers, cabbage, and radishes in big boxes. There we met Shin Chon ajooma, a woman who had worked for my younger aunt and who was now working at the grocery store. She would give us several bags of cabbages so we could make our own kimchi and save our money.

Mother was very sensitive to color. She had used color to express herself in her embroidery, and when she walked the streets she always noted how colorfully American women dressed. It made even elderly women look young and vibrant. She began to dress herself in more daring colors, and was happy to wear them.

Whenever we traveled, we tried to take my mother with us. It was my husband's opinion that we shouldn't leave her home alone. He felt sorry that she had sacrificed so much to come and live with us, and that we ought to try to make her feel welcome and happy. Also, she made it much easier to watch the children.

Soon I became pregnant with a third child. Our apartment would be too small for our family, so we decided to buy a house in Pequannock, where Dr. Chu, who had been working at Jun Ju Ye-soo Hospital, was living. We paid the down payment with the money that my husband earned with his extra hours work. We moved into the new house in 1974, when I was almost due for delivery. My mother liked the house very much because it had a half acre yard where she could garden and cultivate vegetables for us to eat. She always felt a connection to the earth.

She encouraged me to continue my studies, saying there was no need for two women to stay home taking care of children and doing household work. So I started to learn English at William Paterson College, which was 10 minutes from our house. It was due to mother's kind consideration that I could continue my education.

Even though my husband and I did our best to treat my mother well, she still felt uneasy living with us. It became even more stressful for her when my husband's parents came to stay with us without warning, and stayed for about a year and a half without ever detailing their plans to us. During that time my husband's father prepared for his test to become a medical specialist and awaited his youngest daughter Won Sun's high school graduation.

A total of ten people occupied our three bedroom house for two years, and we often clashed.

Even though Mother was living a painfully lonely life, she did not divulge her suffering to anyone. She endured her loneliness and assuaged it only through prayer. Only God understood her lonely life and comforted her.

MOTHER'S INDEPENDENCE

The six years she spent separated from her family in Korea were not easy for my mother. She was able to overcome her difficulties through her own strength and patience.

At last, the family in Korea was making preparations to come to America and reunite with my mother and my own family, but Mother did not want them to live in her son-in-law's house. "Hwain, it seems that your father can come to America within the year. What do you think we should do?"

"Well. . ." I could not answer my mother bluntly, because I knew how sensitive she was. I had to be cautious and watch her response to sense her mood.

"How about getting your own job, mother? I think you can get a job easily if we ask Mr. Choi, the church elder." He was a member of our Bible study group with whom we had spoken many times before, and who seemed very willing to arrange a job for my mother. He was an engineer who consulted many companies. The only problem was that the company at which he secured a position was in upstate New York, an hour drive from our home. I couldn't think of my mother making the long drive to a new area alone. My mother sensed my concern and prepared for her independence.

We began to look for houses where my mother could settle down and start a new life when our family arrived from Korea. We scoured the area in which the company was located, so that my mother could be within 30 minutes walking distance of work. It was an adventure for me to travel around with a real estate agent, and to walk through so many houses, and to see so many views out of the windows. Even though the task required me to drive long distances and struggle to communicate with my poor English, I was glad to do something for my mother who had never hesitated to do anything for me.

I wanted to get the best deal possible for my mother, so I pretended to know a lot more about houses than I actually did, and asked the agent detailed questions. I had to go it alone because my mother needed to stay home and care for our newest child. I drove up while the kids were at school.

I found a suitable house within a week. It was a 3 bedroom, two family house just 10 minutes walking distance from the company where mother would work. It seemed to me that God had guided me to it. I told mother that we should buy the house without hesitation. Mother told me that she brought $30,000 from Korea, which was the maximum limitation—$10,000 per person. We decided to buy the house under my husband's name. We agreed on a total price of $105,000 with $25,000 as a down payment. The rest would be loaned from the bank. We could not buy the house in either of my parents' names, because they had no credit history or jobs in America.

To prepare for the start of her life in her new house, my mother began to learn English. I taught her what she needed to know to live alone.

"Mother, say 'Good morning' when you meet people in the morning. When they say 'How are you?', be sure to reply by saying 'Fine, thank you. How are you?'"

"I know what to say, but I'm not sure if I can actually speak it out."

"Mother, you have to practice speaking it out." In this way, I taught my mother the basics. I also taught her how to answer the phone by practicing a number of different situations with her.

"Mother, what would you do if you lost your way?" I also gave some quizzes to mother. Mother listened motionlessly without knowing how to answer.

"Mother, go to the public phone booth if you don't know where you are. Then dial 0 and my phone number and tell the operator 'collect call please, this is Mrs. Chang.'" I saw my mother's face flush red and her eye open wide with surprise.

"Mother, you can do it." I encouraged her. I knew she was afraid to be left alone to her own devices in this foreign country, but I tried to be positive and support her enthusiastically. I encouraged her to have a self-confidence and not to be embarrassed. I had to pretend not to know how lonely my mother would be without me to prevent tears from filling my eyes. She must have endured more than I could ever have imagined.

Mother at last finished the 6 years and 3 months of her living with me and my family. She moved out and began living at her new house in Mamaroneck. The first night she spent alone in the house was painfully long. The slightest sound roused her and she could not bear to close her eyes.

The telephone rang the next morning at around 6:30. "Mother, it's me. Did you sleep well?" I asked.

Pleased to hear her daughter's voice, my mother replied, "Yes, of course, I slept well."

MOTHER'S NEW WORKPLACE

My mother starting working the day after she arrived at her new home. The only man she knew in town, Mr. Choi worked during the nights, so my mother could not see him during the day because she herself was working. However, Mr. Choi had asked my mother's supervisor and colleagues to treat her well, so they were very kind to her. The company manufacture electronic goods and mother's work required her to pack the small products into bags. It was an easy job. Her employers had taken into consideration her age and language constraints, and gave her a job that did not require that she speak very much. A simple "Good morning" or "Hi" when the supervisor came around sufficed. Most of the workers at the same table as mother were old women in their 60s, 50s or 40s. Mary, who distributed work to my mother liked her because she worked diligently without getting distracted by conversation, as many of the other women. She finished her work efficiently and quickly.

The other women who worked alongside mother resented her efficiency, because it meant they could not slow down or take breaks like they were used to doing. Mother's inability to speak the language of those around her alienated her and made her a target of bitter talk. In Korea she had been a businesswoman and a teacher, but now she was performing menial tasks to eke out a living. Only the thought of her family coming to America sustained her.

As Mother grew accustomed to the work and the workers grew accustomed to her, her frustrations eased. Perhaps people treated her kindly because of her age and her gentleness? Some came over to her and patted her shoulder, saying some greeting. "You, very good, very good," they said. She later realized that they were Italian immigrants who also could not speak English fluently. She was popular among them for her neat and pretty style of dress. I'd bought her bright dresses to cheer her up.

Mother sometimes got up early in the morning at around 4:00 am, even though her actual work began at 8. Upon waking, she decorated her hair and did her makeup tidily, and prepared for the day ahead. She dressed as neatly and professionally as an executive even though she was only a worker packing electronics. Then she prepared for her lunch. She liked rice and kimchi but she was too embarrassed to eat it at work, so she made a very American meal of a sandwich with lettuce and turkey, with a thermos of coffee. She hardly ever left her seat even during break. Her other co-workers would make coffee for. She managed the difficult life of a worker because of the love she received from her fellow co-workers. Her job kept her busy and the fear and discomfort that had accompanied her solitude was mollified.

DIALOGUE IN THE LONELINESS

"Brrrr. . . . . ." The phone rang when mother just came in from the work.

"Mother, it's me. Are you OK?"

"Yes, I just got back from work. I am panting for breath. I ran up the stairs to hear the phone bell."

"How was today, mother?" I asked her worrisomely.

"I am OK. The people are treating me nicely." Mother then talked about everything that happened during the day.

"Mother, it's almost time that my husband comes home. I will hang up now. Have a nice dinner and good evening. Bye, bye."

Mother felt her loneliness grip her suddenly. Even though I had filled her refrigerator with groceries and all the ingredients of the delicacies she loved to cook, she could only bring herself to eat them alone. She set out a bowl of rice and some kimchi and began to eat. That night, she couldn't sleep. She took out her Bible and began to read, thinking of her lovely daughter and her family in Korea.

She had finished the Old Testament and had not long ago begun the New Testament. She was reading Mark. Jesus was on the way to his last cross. He entered Jerusalem and scolded the merchants who disgraced the holy temple by selling wares on its steps. Then Jesus preached to his disciples. He said: "For this reason I tell you: When you pray and ask for something, believe that you have received it, and you will be given whatever you ask for." (Mark, 11:24).

My mother read the verse and began to pray: "Lord, you said you would listen to my every prayer. Please set me free from my suffering. Please let me be with my family soon." My mother remembered that Jesus took the loneliest path of all to save humanity from the sin. She began to pray with mother began to make a conversation with the loneliness of Jesus. Experiencing the deep love of Jesus, the savior, as a worthless human being, mother reconfirmed the confidence of his saying that he is not lonely. The clock already pointed 2:00 am. Mother tried to sleep for the next day.

VII.

Reunion

THE REUNION OF THE FAMILY

THE FAMILY'S MOVE TO the United States had not been easy to accomplish. The children's school matters and the acquisitions of visas and passports all delayed the time of the family's entry into America. Joon had to take his college entrance examination. Hwa Bong wanted to major in the fine arts, for which she had a fine talent, but mother and I strongly objected to it, because it didn't seem like a secure course. We persuaded her instead to go to nursing school, a choice which would ensure a good job in the future. At the time Hwa Bong was a junior at the Yon Sei Nursing School and Joon entered Korea University Business School. When the immigration visas, for which we had waited so long, finally arrived, the children had to decide when to come. Hwa Bong of course had to finish her senior year of nursing school and Joon, then a first year student, would have to transfer. We all had to discuss the matter to find the best solution.

We finally decided that Hwa Bong should wait until her graduation to come to America, and that father Joon, and Hwa Yong should come in advance. Joon was to enter as a senior Mamaroneck High School, and Hwa Young would enter as a junior. The four family members worked hard to adjust to life in America; their new lives had to begin immediately. I spoke to Joon and told him to forget the fact that he had been a college student in Korea. High school in America was just as liberal as colleges, and the students didn't have to wear uniforms. Joon had to have time to adjust to living in America and to take the SATs before attending college there. We didn't give father any opportunity to choose what this new life would hold for him. We set up a job for him at the same company that employed my mother, and he began the very next day after their arrival.

All the members of the family soldiered through the changes like machines. They only wanted to find themselves in a state of some stability or normalcy before they could feel safe enough to lift their heads and feel the lives they were living. Mother and father thanked God for their safe entrance into America and their reunion. Even though they were apart from their closest relatives, their economic independence gave them confidence. My mother and I began to speak less and less on the phone as she became busier with her own life, and as activities and family concerns began to fill out the space that had once been her solitude. Though the work and the strain of adjustment tired her out, she maintained her hope and felt sure that the future held wonderful things for her family. She was thankful that she could work with her husband and finally have someone to speak to there. She only awaited Hwa Bong's arrival. The family was growing accustomed to the new country, and was glad that they had carved out a space in so foreign a place for their own.

THE TRAFFIC ACCIDENT

About two months after the family settled in, my husband bought a car for father. It was a red 6 cylinder Chevy Impala that did not consume too much gas. Father and mother came to visit us at our home in New Jersey. I rode with him several times until he became more familiar with the roads. They visited one weekend, and we went to church and had dinner together. It was windy and rainy that night, so we advised them to stay the night and leave for work early in the morning. They left when it was still dark, at about 5 am in the heavy fog that lingered after the downpour. They left Pequannock and took Route 80. When they reached the George Washington Bridge they found that the mist off of the river was much thicker than on the highway, and the other cars were hardly visible. They barely passed the bridge and just came out to the exit to Route 95 when mother realized they had gone the wrong way. Just as she told my father, he stepped on the break and swerved the car to the side. Just then, a big passenger car barreling forward hit the front of father's car. After the impact, the driver ran over and said words that neither of my parents could understand. A police car arrived and my parents were taken to a nearby hospital.

At 6 o'clock in the morning when I woke, I found that they had already left. In my mind I worried that the fog would be dangerous. I took my kids to school and the worry weighed heavy in chest. I was anxious to hear from them but I had to wait until they got off work.

"Hello, Is there a Mrs. Lee there?" I received a phone call from a man.

"Yes, this is she." I replied.

"This is the New York Police Department." The man's voice continued, but I don't remember the words that came after. A gloomy foreboding slid over me. The policeman told me that my father and mother were hospitalized in the emergency room of New York Hospital after a traffic accident on the highway. Even though the policeman said repeatedly that my parents were not severely injured, my heart almost stopped beating. I immediately called my husband in Chilton Hospital and told him that I was going to the New York Hospital.

The emergency room of the hospital was crowded. Interns and residents skittered hastily between the beds, policemen marched in and out, and all kinds of people waited to hear about their injured loved ones. I searched for my parents and found them both wearing oxygen masks. It seemed to me their condition was more severe than the policeman, who was waiting for me, had indicated. I sensed immediately that he had only wanted to comfort me. When I asked him how the other driver was doing he said that the driver of the limousine was not injured and that he had been discharged after a few tests.

The nurses and doctors were visiting father. He was the one driving and seemed to be the one more severely injured as a result. I reported back to my husband the details of the situation, and then arranged for the doctor in charge of my parents to talk to him directly. I told the news about my parents' accidents to Mr. Choi and Mr. Sohn, the elders of our church, who had become as close to as family members. They had loved mother so tenderly, and taken care of her since her arrival in the US.

After about three hours, my parents were moved out of the ER to a private room. I kept watch over my father and tried to chart any changes in his condition. Even with my minimal medical knowledge, I felt strongly that the doctors shouldn't be pumping so many unnecessary drugs into my father's system. I observed his face closely and saw that his head and nose had swollen, but his voice was clear. My mother was doing ok, but my father's EKG had shown troublesome results.

After a while, father began to speak to me and to complain of a pain in his arm. His voice became vague and faint until he couldn't speak anymore. He pointed weakly to the needle in his arm and signaled to me that he wanted it removed. His face distorted with pain. I ran to the pay phone and paged my husband, who called back immediately.

"Honey, father's speech is abnormal and he's signaling that the IV on his arm is hurting him. What should I do? I think the Lidocaine is causing complications."

"Mmmm, it's possible," he answered level-headedly. "I'll talk to their doctor. You stay by his side."

I ran back to father's room after hanging up the phone. I called the nurse and told her my father wanted the IV removed, that it was hurting him, but she said she couldn't do anything without the doctor's express consent. For about 30 to 40 minutes, I watched my father suffer his pain. At last, a resident came and stopped the drug and started him on a new IV with only the basic liquid. After that, father returned to a normal condition.

After this incident, I wanted to transfer my parents out of the hospital as soon as possible. I decided to move father to the Chilton Hospital, where my husband was working. I thought it would be better to have him nearby, so I could get home easily and look after my children and still see him often. It took more than an hour to prepare for the ambulance. We had to call a private ambulance to take him across state lines. Our case was expedited by the fact that my husband was a medical doctor.

I followed after the ambulance carrying my parents and arrived at the hospital after 9 o'clock in the evening. I felt at home in Chilton Hospital. I arranged for them to have a private room due to the language barrier, and I returned home, my whole body exhausted.

WITH THE SECOND DAUGHTER

The last member of our family to arrive was Hwa Bong, the second daughter. During mother's ten weeks stay at the hospitals, her daughter's letters from Korea brought her much comfort. My mother had parted with her daughter when she was a girl in high school with hair cut to her chin, and now she had grown to be a women who was graduating college. Hwa Bong was different in nature than I was—she was fastidious and introspective. Mother like to have long, detailed conversations with her. She had raised me to be a kind of rock of stability, and in Hwa Bong she found a friend with whom she could share warm conversations. Because I was married and had my own family to care for, my mother hoped that her second daughter would be able to live in their home and help her with housework. Her time in the hospital made the time of waiting pass easily, lazily by. She only waited for her daughter to come to America.

Hwa Bong had good news upon her graduation—she was graduating with top honors. My mother shed tears of joy. She was thankful that Hwa Bong had succeeded on her own in Korea without her mother during the ling years of their separation. She regretted not being able to witness it herself. When it was time to immigrate, Hwa Bong gave my mother a list of what she would need, and brought with her all the items that mother asked for.

With the addition of Hwa Bong, the savings of the family gradually increased. Joon and Hwa Young attended public school so there was little expense between the two of them. The money saved was used to buy groceries and other necessities. With the entire family finally reunited, things began to settle down. Hwa Bong decided to work at the same company as her parents while she prepared for the registered nurse test, and while she grew accustomed to the new country. The three bedroom, two family house became mother's new nest of love.

THE PLEASURE OF GROCERY SHOPPING

One of my parent's sweetest pleasures was going grocery shopping with Hwa Bong. Hwa Bong could read and speak English, so they no longer had to be embarrassed at their own inabilities. Hwa Bong could do anything for them now. They had much more freedom at work, because they could call Hwa Bong at any time when they had difficulty communicating with others.

Mother and father went to the A & P, the biggest grocery in their town, for their grocery shopping. They were amazed at the freshness and abundance of food. It was much cheaper here than in Korea, where they had buy at high price things that were imported from America. They could buy as much American coffee, bar soap, sausage, bacon, and butter as they wanted. A cart-full of groceries was less than $100. Melons and grapefruit were special favorites of my parents. There had been none in Korea. Buying Korean groceries was another small pleasure. There was a Korean grocery at White Plains where they would go after work or on the weekends to buy tofu, bean sprouts, and ingredients for kimchi. The luxuries of Korea seemed so plentiful and affordable here.

Vacationing and shopping are said to be the two greatest pleasures of American life. Mother and her family took great joy in their shopping. While in Korea they had to bargain for good prices, here could buy at designated prices with satisfaction. For father who liked to buy good merchandise, America was good place to live. Sale items could be bought here at less than half price.

Mother began to fully enjoy her life in America for the first time. She prayed to God every night and early every morning to thank him for all the pleasures he gave them here.

A SON BECAME COLLEGE STUDENT

Mother's decision to have Joon repeat his high school senior year proved a wise move. He was able to learn English and study for the SAT. Even though his English scores were not excellent, he got a perfect score in math. It must have been easy for him compared to the material he had learned in Korea. When Joon applied to colleges, all the family members discussed his future seriously. We had to choose a state university that was not too expensive, and one that was not too far from us. My parents grieved at the thought of having to part with him again. Joon decided to attend the State University of New York at Albany with the unanimous consent of our family members. He worked part time when he was not studying, earning pocket money and giving mother the rest of what he earned.

Joon graduated high school with good grades and made us proud by receiving an award for his academic achievement. Mother felt that her efforts on behalf of her children had been successful and thanked to God for everything. She believed that the traffic accident was a warning to be careful with the life that had been given her. She decided to live cautiously.

Each member of the family performed his or her share of the housework from morning until night. My parents, Hwa Bong, and Joon worked hard and their savings increased. No one wasted money. They knew that the savings would be used some day for some important thing, so no one complained. Their cooperation as one unit gave each of them a feeling of security.

HWA BONG, THE NURSE

The date of Hwa Bong's test to become a registered nurse drew near. Mother sensed that Hwa Bong became very sensitive because of all the stress of studying, and fear of not performing well. She understood that her daughter felt uneasy, and that the strain caused her to quarrel with her brother and sister. Mother made every effort to reconcile them. She played the mediator and tried impossibly to read her children's minds and give each of them what they wanted.

Even after a long day's work, she prepared dinner for her family alone in the kitchen. She did not ask her daughters to help her because she loved them, and as a son, Joon was not permitted to do kitchen work. After the accident, Father preferred not to drive, Hwa Bong and Joon helped their mother with the grocery shopping.

Hwa Bong was always a self-motivated student, so mother didn't worry about her passing the test. Hwa Bong was completely engrossed in her studying, and forgot to think of others. Mother tried to understand and to accept her daughter's nervous as the test approached. Mother could suffer anything that had good cause. She told her daughter to have confidence and belief.

"Hwa Bong, you will surely pass the test. You were an honor student." Mother encouraged her.

All the family members were pleased when Hwa Bong's test was finished. She didn't have to work at Sealectro anymore, because her added qualification made her eligible for a higher salary. I asked Hwa Bong to come to my home, and urged her to work a nursing home in our town where she could learn English and grow accustomed to nursing. Hwa Bong heeded my advice and decided to work as a nursing aid until she received her license. She lived with me for several months and, like my mother, made sure never to disturb us or to ask too much of us. She walked the 20 minutes to the nursing home so that no one had to drive her.

Hwa Bong learned a lot from her experience as a nursing aid. She was careful to fulfill all the expectations of her employers, as this was her first time in the professional world. She worked the evening shift from three o'clock in the afternoon to eleven o'clock at night. She slept late into the morning.

A LAWSUIT FOR THE TRAFFIC ACCIDENT

The 10 years she spent with her family at Mamaroneck were the happiest of her life. The tensions, fears, and anxieties that arose at her work did not follow her home. With time, father's skill and mother's kindness made them popular at work. Mother made friends with the neighbors and often visited them.

Her youngest daughter entered college and her son graduated and entered medical school, which was every immigrant's dream. Hwa Bong worked as a nurse at New Rochelle Hospital near mother's home and married the brother-in-law of the church elder Mr. Choi.

One day a letter written in English came in the mail. "Joon, what is this letter?" My mother asked, handing the piece of paper to her son who had just returned from school.

"This is addressed to my brother-in-law. It looks like to be about the traffic accident."

"Then, I have to call your sister right now."

"Mother, this is from the lawyer's office." Joon said, squinting at the letter. "Somebody is suing brother-in-law for compensation because of the traffic accident."

Mother was shocked. She had always tried to avoid burdening her son-in-law. When I got her call, my brother explained to me the meaning of the letter. The limousine driver had filed a suit, claiming he had lost his job and suffered issues in his sexual life because of the accident. My parents were appalled that they were being accused of some misconduct when they themselves had been the injured parties. Perhaps my father had made a mistake while driving, but the heavy fog had exacerbated the situation, and no blame, they felt, ought to fall on themselves. Mother could not understand the situation. She lost sleep from all her worrying.

My husband remained calm. He told me not to worry, because we did nothing wrong. But my mother could not face her son-in-law because she felt she was responsible for imposing all the confusion and stress of the lawsuit on my family. The lawyer's deposition started and requests for pleading at the bar began to arrive. Father and mother said that they would do anything that could help their son-in-law. They learned how to be cautious in their speech. Because they still were not fluent in English, I worried that there would be some misunderstanding during trial. I asked my parents just to answer questions with a simple "yes" or "no."

The trial took almost 2 years to complete. It made our lives during that time uneasy. Just when we were about to move on and forget about the case, we received another letter reminding us. Mother felt that the America law system was corrupted. It functioned only to trap people and not to serve any kind of justice. She felt sorry that her son-in-law had to bear the brunt of the accusations.

As the lawsuit progressed, Bill began to become concerned. The amount of money the plaintiff was demanding was constantly rising and the case was becoming more and more complicated. Our insurance company said that we didn't have to worry. They said it shouldn't even be a case. But the plaintiff submitted several different doctors' diagnoses and claimed he suffered endless physical and spiritual damages. At last the amount of the suit went up to one million dollars. We were dumbfounded. My husband appointed his personal lawyer and he requested that the insurance company settle the case. But the insurance company was confident that they would win. At last, the insurance company tried to shift the blame onto my husband as the claims amount surpassed their limitation. Bill told his story to his long time lawyer friend Mr. Bob Galo, who told us that the insurance company was totally wrong. He renounced the insurance company for its negligence in rejecting the settlement and for not considering their client's best interest. The insurance company at last decided to settle the case and ended up paying three times the initial claim amount. Even though we didn't have to pay, we were left with a deep distrust of the American legal system. I wondered whether there was actually any progress in a nation that made claims to such advancement.

PREPARATION FOR RETIREMENT

Mother's everyday life got back to normal. The feeling of uneasiness regarding the suit began to disappear after the proceedings finally ended. Mother took great pleasure in hearing that the case was at last closed. She could now return to normalcy and concentrate on her work and family.

Her 60th birthday party was a grand affair held at my house. All the church members attended.

All the family members were registered at the Bronx Korean Presbyterian Church. My husband was an elder of the church and mother had been a member since she first came to America. Mother was confirmed as a deacon not long after her arrival. She participated eagerly in the various church groups such as the collection committee, the women's group, and the bazaar organization committee. She served with a full heart and with abounding faith, because she wanted to give to her God and to her family.

Father didn't have a choice when it came to finally selecting a church. He had to follow the rest of his family to do so. He often quarreled with mother about attending, but mother asked him to come for his daughter. This was my mother's only weapon in swaying her husband's resolve.

Mother had Hwa Bong, Joon, and Hwa Young baptized as Christians. With relish, she felt her prayers being accomplished little by little as the years passed. She was especially thankful that Hwa Bong was married into the family of Mr. Choi, whose belief in God was so firm. She thanked God for giving her a son-in-law who was sincere and who would found his family on firm belief. She also thanked God for Joon finishing college and attending medical school without financial help from his parents.

Mother began to feel that her body weakening with age. She began to think of retirement. She knew that she would be eligible for the social security benefits if she had worked for more than 8 years. Mother, however, decided to wait until father became 65 years old so that they could retire together. Mother and father worked very hard, and often worked extra hours when the workload was especially big. It amused them to save their money and watch their savings rise. Hwa Bong had prepared for her marriage with her own savings and Jon was receiving student loans to cover the cost of medical school. Hwa Young was also living independently. With all these blessings, mother and father were very satisfied and happy with their lives in America. They only retired after their children urged them to do so.

"Honey, don't you think we should move to New Jersey?" Mother asked her husband.

"I agree with you. Then we can help Hwain." Father also thought it natural that they move to New Jersey. He thought it would be better for all of the family members.

"Then, let's discuss the matter with Hwain."

VIII.

New Jersey

MOVING TO NEW JERSEY

A FAREWELL PARTY WAS held for my parents at the company. My parents had become close friends with their colleagues during the period of their work together. Everyone prepared small presents for them. Some brought little homemade cakes as offerings of friendship and congratulation. Even though they could not communicate very well with the other employees, they were deeply loved for their sincerity and hard work. Many envied them the freedom of retirement, and their move to New Jersey to be with their child.

My parents rented out their New York house, then moved to an elegant old house in New Jersey more than 200 years old in Franklin Lakes. It was the house of one of my husband's patients. It had a large property of 2 and a half acres. The road in front of the house was named Pulis, after the man who had first lived there. There were two rooms on the second floor and a living room, a dining room, and a kitchen on the ground floor. It suited my parents who no longer had children to house. Father liked to garden, and to sit out on warm days. Nearby at end of the long narrow sidewalk, was an antique house made of stone, with small peering windows. The highway 287 was going to be built nearby, which would increase the property value. The former owner of the neighboring house had been an antique clock collector who was retiring to Florida. He and his wife wanted desperately to sell their home so they could leave.

Mother and father enjoyed their little nook in the woods and their proximity to their daughter' house. It had been a long time since they lived on their own. Father worked outside in the garden and mother decorated the house's interior. They foresaw wonderful years ahead.

VACATION HOME AT LONG LAKE

One of the things my mother enjoyed most was visiting our lake house in Long Lake in upstate New York. The house is nestled on one of the banks of the lake, which takes about an hour and a half to ride the length of by motor boat. We bought the lake house the same year we purchased out first home. Every Memorial Day weekend, we all drove out for our most anticipated gathering of the year. My parents, who prepared the house for the rest of us, opened all the windows that had been sealed shut through the cold winter. Warm, vital air would sweep through the stuffy rooms. My mother cleaned and my father decorated the windows with boxes of red geraniums. He filled all the flower boxes in the woodshed with bright summer flowers and cleared the dead branches and leaves from the porch, saying that maybe the neighbors would like it instead.

The black flies that swarm around Long Lake in the summer reach their peak around the end of May. They stick to sweat-damp skin and suck blood. Mother and I mainly cleaned inside the house, but father ventured to clean the outside of the house despite the black flies.

Father loved to fish and when the sun rose he was already in the middle of the lake in a canoe. He caught bass, yellow perch, and catfish, then cleaned them by the lakeside. We cooked them with a little salt and made stew with soy bean and red pepper pastes. The smell of the food drifted through all the rooms and out toward the water.

Father enjoyed the work that tending to the house required. When the logs of the log house turned black, he scraped them clean with sandpaper under the warm sun until they showed chestnut brown again. There was no corner or cranny of the place that father didn't touch and care for. He designated places for hanging his fishing rods and the motor boat safety cushion, and even a place for hanging all his cleaning tools. Every mess untangled and smoothed out beneath his hands.

My children called him the best, most creative handyman in the world. My second child even wrote an essay about how wise his grandfather was. At the age of 70, he could still swim at pace with his grandsons. Mother always thanked God for his health.

My mother and father wanted to be independent so that they would not be a burden on their children. At Long Lake, they could feel the worth and openness of their lives. It was a place where they could enjoy all that they had acquired in their long lives—their grandchildren, their wisdom, their comfort.

SENIOR CITIZEN'S ASSOCIATION

Mother and father joined the Korean Senior Citizens Association as soon as they moved to New Jersey. Regular meetings were held every second Tuesday with about 150 members attending from all over the state. Lunch provided by Korean churches was served. Mother and father became directors of the association, and father also served as secretary. He became fast friends with many of the members, whom he visited frequently. He could still drive and so serve those who couldn't. Father shared sesame leaves, cucumbers, and tomatoes from his garden with his friends. He was grateful that he could live in America while still maintaining a Korean lifestyle and enjoying the company of people who shared his cultural background.

"Hwain? We are going to go on a group trip," Mother told me one day during one of our phone conversations.

"Where are you going?" I asked.

"We are going to Niagara Falls. On the way we're planning to stop at the Saratoga Cave and several other places."

"Is that so? Are you going too?"

"No. I want to speak with you so I decided not to join them."

"Why not? This is a good opportunity for you. I know you've been there, but father hasn't." It was then she told me her concern that she urinated too frequently, and worried that a long car ride would prove uncomfortable for her. I told my mother not to worry, that I would ask Bill to prescribe her something.

I felt relieved that my parents had the opportunity to go on a trip with friends their age. It was already autumn, and the trees along the road would be bursting with new colors. Mother and father were excited for the trip and planned for several days. They began to think about what food to take with them, but lamented that their friends didn't have daughters or daughters-in-law to prepare meals for them too. Then my mother came up with an idea.

"Let's make food bags!" It was a good idea. My mother always took great care to prepare food beautifully and neatly. I bought candy and nuts to fill out the sandwich bags, just as we did when the nursery kids went on a trip. We tied the bags shut with little pink ribbons and secured stickers on each on which we wrote my parents' names.

Their life was as full of surprises and pleasures to be savored as that of a newly married couple. Father treated my mother more tenderly than he had in the earlier years of their marriage, and joked that he would make it all up to her now. My mother accepted these unexpected years of joy as a last, wonderful gift from God.

A TRIP TO JERUSALEM

Not long after the trip to the Niagara Falls, our church in Bronx planned a trip to Jerusalem for its senior members. Mother and father joined the minister and his wife as well as ten other members embarked for Jerusalem on March 20, 1990. Their two weeks travel time included a stop in Rome, a prospect which filled my mother with anticipation. Mother, who had read the entire Bible, left Kennedy airport with the thrill of a child journeying to meet the hero of her most cherished stories.

The history of the Bible spread out before them—real and tangible—as the minister guided them from place to place, detailing at each all the events in the Bible that had taken place there. Mother had imagined that the Red Sea and the Jerusalem Castle would be enormous, because of the enormity of their importance in her faith. But she counted that they were different from what she expected. When she trekked up the hill of Golgotha, she was somewhat disappointed at the change that had occurred over the 2000 years that separated her time from that of Jesus. The place had become too commercialized. Still, my mother felt the presence of Jesus lingering there despite the time past and the changes exacted, and the experience brought her closer to him.

Father was the quickest and healthiest of the seniors; he led the way with his swift steps and helped the other seniors with their baggage. Mother began to connect with the other members and with the minister who traveled with her. Although they attended the same church, they knew little of each other before the trip. Her heart was convicted with the desire to build relationships with the Christians around her. It was so difficult to know people and to understand their hearts and minds, and she resolved to open herself to understanding.

The wife of the minister also took special care of my mother and father. She knew very well that mother had lived apart from her family for very long and had worked hard to bring everyone together again. The minister also loved my mother. He often comforted and encouraged her through her difficulties. His style of treating his members was decidedly different that those other ministers who presided over big churches. He never lost sight of the individuals within the great mass of the congregation.

This trip made my mother and father feel as though their world had been burst open. They now felt that their vision had expanded to encompass this new piece of the world. My mother made a scrapbook of the picture my father took, and wrote little captions beneath each of them so she could remember every moment, every sight in detail. The two volumes she created remain in my family's care.

THE 70TH BIRTHDAY PARTY

Mother was a year older than Father. We threw her a lavish 70th birthday party at our house and invited all of our friends and church members. An artist names Kyu Nam Han made a huge banner that read: "Congratulations on your 70th birthday, Ms. Yun Ae Kyun Kwonsa." We hung it up in the grand room and beneath it we arranged a huge table brimming with food.

Father's 70th birthday party was quite different than Mother's. Mother took initiative in planning the party. She had been reluctant to let us throw hers, but now that she was celebrating her husband, she threw herself into the festivities. She wanted to hold it in her own house, and we children all agreed. Hwa Bong, Joon, his wife Sung Ja, and Hwa Young all said that they would gladly perform whatever tasks were assigned them. We started preparations a full month before the party. We sent out invitations, reserved tents, chairs, and tables for all the guests. Joon got off work a week before the party and came with his wife to help set up.

The preparations were moving along smoothly, though I wasn't actively involved. I thought it better that I stand back and watch my brothers and sisters at work, taking charge. I just did whatever they needed me to do. Mother ordered traditional Korean costumes for all of her children, including her sons-in-law. All the married women wore dark blue skirts with light blue jackets, and the unmarried women wore red skirts with striped rainbow jackets. Mother tended to every detail; she even planted flowers at the entrance of the house.

It was June 16, and the flowers were in full bloom. We decorated the entire house with rosy blooms that steeped the place in sweet smells. In May, Mother had planted pink and white begonia all around the yard. The New Jersey Korean Senior Citizen's Association sent a wreath and the New Jersey YWCA sent a bouquet. The YWCA was especially thankful to father for allowing them to use his barn as an office and classroom for SAT preparation.

The party was a great success. It finished with a special service presided over by Minister Sung Hyun Lee. All of my father's children congratulated each other on all the effort they had invested in the celebration. We were proud that we had all come together to create something for our father. We thanked God for blessing us with one another.

THE DEATH OF MATERNAL GRANDMOTHER

Hwa Young, who had spent several months in Korea during her summer vacation, told mother that she had made a friend—a nice young man who loved her and asked her to marry him. He wanted to follow her to the US, and marry her in the spring. Mother was pleased to hear the news, but worried about her daughter's choice. She had never met the man. Mother had bought two-tone Rolex watches for her new son-in-law's when they got engaged, and she prepared one of the same for this new addition to the family. Hwa Young is the most gentle and kind of her four children. She was independent in nature, and never gave anyone trouble. Mother felt sorry that she had missed so much of Hwa Young's young life when they had been apart.

While we were preparing for Hwa Young's engagement, we received a phone call from Korea. One of my cousins called to tell my mother that grandmother had fallen seriously ill. Mother prepared to leave for Seoul immediately. Perhaps she had a premonition of her mother's death. She regretted how rarely she was able to see her mother over the past few years. Grandmother was already 95 years old, and she had lost half of her consciousness long time ago. She could not control her body and she had stayed at the home of her eldest daughter, where her grandson cared for her.

Grandmother could no longer practice her faith, and was now living as burden on her daughter and grandson. My mother had always felt guilty that she had found happiness in America while her mother suffered back home. She regretted that she was not around to be with her. My father had a difficult relationship with grandmother, and preferred not to see her at all. My mother knew very well that this tension existed, and that it prohibited her from welcoming grandmother into her new life, no matter how much she desired to have her near.

My mother wanted to see grandmother before she died. She wanted to meet her two sister again under one roof. They had lost touch over the years as they'd grown older and chosen different paths. But when my mother arrived, she found that grandmother had already died. The funeral was large and attended by many. The three sisters shared in the small joy of their reunion as they mourned their mother's passing. Once again they departed, each going her own way again.

THE GUEST, THE IN-LAWS

Hwa Young introduced her fiancé to our family. He planned to begin his studies in America and work to earn a living at the same time. We had a dinner and welcomed the young man into our family. It was a blessing that my mother's four children had now brought four more to share our love. All of us rejoiced that Hwa Young now had someone she loved and who would take care of her.

The date of engagement ceremony was set by the parents of the bridegroom. The father of bridegroom could not come because of his work, so his mother arrived with two friends instead, three days before the ceremony. It was held out our house and began with a brief engagement worship presided over by the minister. The two families exchanged gifts. Hwa Young's mother -in-law gave many presents to her new daughter-in-law. We joked that the presents become nicer as time goes by. We soon became acquainted with Hwa Young's mother-in-law, speaking of marriage and all its joys.

Hwa Young busily hosted her mother-in-law and her friends who were visiting America for the first time. She travelled with them and did her best to show them the country. Mother worried a little bit about Hwa Young's attitude, but she felt proud to see her serving her mother-in-law so dutifully.

TRADITIONAL KOREAN WEDDING CEREMONY

We were all caught up in the excitement of the upcoming wedding. Hwa Bong and I compared the gifts we had received from our in-laws to Hwa Young's lavish presents, and were pleased to find that she, the youngest, had received the most. Her in-laws were very kind to her. Mother was busy buying presents to present to Hwa Young's parents-in-law and new husband.

The wedding ceremony was to be held in Seoul, so the whole family travelled there, full of anticipation. Normally, the wedding reception was planned by the bride's family, but because we lived in America, Hwa Young's in-laws took care of everything. I arrived in Seoul a day before the ceremony with my youngest daughter.

The ceremony was held in Kimpo, a suburb of Seoul, where the groom's father worked. The reception was held at the largest local restaurant with food prepared by the family of the bridegroom. All the traditional Korean foods were served—Bulgogi, Chapche, Jeon and Kuksoo. We ate seated on the Ondol. Mother was dressed in a beautiful Hanbok and was honored by all the guests. My mother, father, the bride, the bridegroom, and his parents were all seated at same table, and we were seated at the family table.

We watched the bowing ceremony in which the newlyweds bow to the groom's parents and relatives. The bride bowed first to her husband's parents, who then threw fistfuls of Chinese dates and asked her to give birth to a healthy grandson. It was an old belief that if the bride eats Chinese dates on the night of her wedding, she will give birth to a healthy boy. Hwa Young followed all these traditional procedures, and when the ceremony finished she had a bruise on her forehead. I always found those ceremonies baffling. It was always the women who bent their bodies to the floor and never the men.

THE SPRING CARE OF THE HOUSE

Things returned to normal after Hwa Young's wedding ceremony. The fresh air of May cleared our minds. Mother and father, returning home from a month of travelling in Seoul, busied themselves

rearranging the house for summer. Father usually began gardening just after the snow of winter melted, but his daughter's wedding had delayed all normal activity, so he began as soon as they
returned. He worked in the early mornings, even when the air bit
with chill. He started to work from early in the morning despite
the chilly air. Their travels had excited them, and even as they resumed life at home, they talked continually of all the things they
had done and seen when they were away.

"I want to cultivate the vegetables nicely this year." said my
father.

"But you have to think about your age," my mother urged
anxiously. "You had better work so hard. Don't overstrain yourself
by making a garden that's too big to care for."

"Don't worry, I won't attempt the impossible. By the way I
was thinking of getting that wood stump by the railroad as a bor-
der for the garden. What do you think of that?" The wood blocks
used during the construction of the railroads were put beside the
work after the work was completed. Father was always looking for
interesting things to beautify his garden. He began to move the
big wood blocks from the side of the railroad and carry them to
our yard. Father's land was about 2.5 acers of dense wood. Father
made a big lever to dislodge the blocks from the earth, but the
work proved too difficult and he quit after two days.

In the soil of his garden, my father planted tomatoes, cucumbers and pumpkins as in previous years, but decided not to seed
the green onions and sesame plants. He drove to the wholesale
nursery near our old house in Pequannock and bought flower
trees to plant at my house and along the pathway of his own. It
took him just two days. Father worked almost all day outside in his
garden, and only came in when dinner was ready.

"Ah, I sprinkled water to the lawn. It is too dry nowadays." he
would say at the table.

IX.

Stroke

UNEXPECTED HAPPENING

"Honey, what's wrong with you?" my mother asked her husband. He had pulled the car over onto the shoulder of Highway 208 near the Route 4. He was blinking hard and rubbing his eyes. Father wondering why he stopped the car suddenly and pulled it to the shoulder.

"I can't see very well, but it may be OK soon."

"Honey, I think you are too tired. Don't work so hard." Mother advised father.

They returned home safely, but father continued to seem unwell. He said he felt dizzy when he stood up and walked around. Sometimes he lost his balance for a few seconds before recovering.

Mother called me and gave me a list of his detailed symptoms. Father had been treating his high blood pressure with the medicine that his son-in-law prescribed. I spoke to my husband immediately, and he arranged an appointment with a neurologist. I escorted father and mother to the hospital the next day. Father took a CT, an MRI and other necessary tests. For three days we waited anxiously for the results to reach us. Father looked as though her were in perfect health and had always lived vigorously, even as he grew older. Finally, my husband gave us the news that the test results had shown no discernible problems with my father's health. We were all relieved, and father became more cautious.

Two months passed. I escorted guests from Seoul to the Long Lake on Independence Day. I had asked my sister and brother to take care of their father, even though he seemed fine at the time. I left home without a doubt that I would return to see him healthy, just as I'd left him. The phone rang in the night. When I answered, the voce on the line said, "Sister, it's me, Joon. Father is in bad shape. We're taking him to emergency room."

"What? How he is?" I shouted. The lake house was dark and quiet. The others were asleep.

"We don't know, but his left shoulder seems to be paralyzed. We are taking him to the Valley Hospital."

"O.K., Please be careful with him. I can't go down now, but I will be there tomorrow."

I felt my heart fell to my knees. I couldn't sleep.

Father was hospitalized that night. My husband asked his colleague doctors to take special care of him. Because his son Joon was also a doctor, we believed his treatment wouldn't be a problem and awaited a speedy recovery from whatever ailed him.

FATHER HAD STROKE

Father had no sensation his left arm and leg. He had had a stroke. Mother was full of despair, and nothing relieved her. She could do nothing for her husband but be with him and watch while the doctors treated him.

Joon spent 3 nights at his father's side, almost without sleeping. He was used to spending his nights in the hospital. The doctors—the best we could find—began to treat him, but nothing seemed to undo the effects of the stroke, or to prevent his condition from deteriorating even further. He lost his ability to speak, and soon the right side of his body became paralyzed too. More tests found that the central blood vessel in his brain had clogged. No treatment seemed to be working. My mother watched as her husband lost the functions of his body one by one. She was all eyes, all anxiety. She drifted among us, pale and speechless.

Hwa Bong secured a week's break from her work as a nurse and visited her father. She cared for him dutifully, with tears standing in her eyes. As she washed his body, she hid her face from the rest of us. She tried to feed him but his throat had become paralyzed as well. None of us looked each other in the eyes.

One by one, each of us had to return to the demands of our own lives, which persisted ruthlessly. Life refused to pause for our suffering, and went resolutely onward. Hwa Bong's vacation could not be extended more than two weeks and Joon, who was a doctor in the middle of his training, had to return to his hospital.

Mother had to return home without Father. The house seemed so large in his absence, and she had to check that the door was locked several times a night. The world and the house that had been so full of bodily warmth had suddenly gone dark and cold. She did not know how to live without her husband. However, she did not lose hope. She believed absolutely that their separation was only a temporary one, and that all this was only a trial she had to overcome to meet him again on the other side. He would eventually recover, she was sure. She had only to care for him in the interim.

After a few weeks, the doctors tactfully informed us that a patient could not be sustained indefinitely on IV injections. They asked us to decide whether to give Father an operation that would allow nutrients to be sent directly into his stomach. It would allow him to be fed through a tube that led into his stomach.

"We have a similar patient in this hospital who is the father of one our nurses," my husband told me. "She decided not to give him the operation, and to let him die peacefully. Maybe it would be better for the patient himself."

We spoke all night without sleeping. My husband called Dr. Ma, who was a specialist in rehabilitation, and his wife Dr. Cho to ask what chance there was of a recovery. "It depends on the patient, but this is a very difficult case. His whole body is paralyzed." I heard the doctor say.

"What do you think we should do?" my husband asked.

Dr. Cho said, "Once the life ends, you cannot retrieve it. It would be better to have a father who is sick than no father at all. Once he dies there's no bringing him back."

We decided to consult my mother. I tried my best to explain the situation to her clearly, and with care not to hurt her.

"I can't let father die" she replied.

"We have to try to the end."

"It will be a long battle, mother. We all have to be ready for that." I found that I myself was making a decision.

"I know," mother replied.

We decided to give father the operation. Catheters and needles were put into his body. Father tried to say something with his eyes, but we couldn't understand.

FATHER RETURNED HOME

My husband had advised us that it was best that Father stay in the hospital as long as possible, even though it was difficult for my mother to commute there, because the care he would receive would be the most qualified. However, he had been in the hospital for three months, and the doctors instructed us that it was time to take him home. Before his discharge, we heard that the father of the nurse who was suffering from the same illness had died.

The family prepared the house for my father's arrival. We rented an automatic bed like the ones in the hospital and rearranged the living room to house a patient, stocking it with gauze and towels. Hwa Bong and Joon obtained the necessary medical equipment. They even got hospital pads and a gown.

Thus, mother welcomed father to a changed home. At first she was afraid that something would go wrong and that she wouldn't know what to do. But with time she became accustomed to her responsibilities. She took Father's urine and checked his temperature and blood pressure regularly. She wrote all of the numbers and notes on a pad. Mother was neat and reserved by nature, and felt uneasy washing her husband's body. She wanted to take her time and clean every inch of him. She washed him tenderly, always smiling.

The physical therapist came over twice a week and the occupational therapist came over once a week. The therapists performed their jobs enthusiastically and did their best for the patient. Though she could not communicate with them, my mother tended assiduously to her visitors while doing her own work around the house. She was grateful to them for caring for her husband.

Father seemed more rested and comfortable in his home. His consciousness became clearer and he was able to express his thoughts. Mother massaged his legs and arms continuously and to prevent his body from stiffening. Father moved his body little by little. He wanted to show us that he could.

> Father!
> I didn't know that
> You are living in this world with us
> Gave us such a strength
> As somebody advised that
> A father that lie in bed
> Is better that the one
> Who is dead.
>
> I thank God that
> I can communicate with you
> Through your eyes and heart.
>
> On every move of your eyes,
> I still feel your deep love of me.
>
> If not these communications with you,
> I would have lost my hope already.

Father, how good it is that
We still have our hope.

Father,
Until the last moment
Let us not give up our hope.

MOTHER'S HANDS

I watched my mother massage her husband's legs each day. Her hands were still lovely, even though they had toiled all the 70 years she had lived. Those hands had knit pretty satins with twisted silk threads for years in her factory. Thousands of little dolls had been fashioned by those little fingers. Those hands had placed my shoes by the kitchen stove to warm there on cold winter nights; they had assembled my lunches each day I went to school; they had tickled and primped and caressed three grandchildren. Even now, their work was to care for others. I thought of mothers like her who devote their lives to the work, the labor of loving.

Hands that moved and strained by day, she folded together at night in prayer. Mother knew the limits that human beings cannot overcome. Only prayer could stir miracles into reality. She believed the stories in the Bible of impossible cures, impossible resurrections. Each night she made her supplications to God to heal her husband, her hands clasped and lifted above her head. When she slept, she dreamed that her husband moved again at last, and was sure that this was God's promise.

MEDICARE

Doctors had told us there wasn't much hope. Father's condition showed no sign of improvement despite our prayers and efforts. My mother cared for him diligently. She couldn't sleep for more than three or four hours a day because his sleeping pills lasted for only a short amount of time. He'd wake in the middle of the night and require my mother's attention. As soon as she heard a noise, she shot up and rushed to his bedside tried to discern what it was he needed. When he coughed or made a sudden jerk, his legs or arms shifted to different position. My mother would have to wake and rearrange his body for him, to spare him discomfort.

Father's care commanded everything of my mother. She had no spirit nor energy to expend lamenting or longing for times past. Sentimentalism offered her no sustenance, no comfort. Every moment was urgent and enormous; she thought of nothing but present demands.

The medical system was of great help to mother. Medicare covered 80 % of the medical bill. The doctors who were friends of my husband treated Father and charged only the insurance covered portion. However, when the support provided by Medicare expired, all the people who came regularly to the house to care for my father stopped coming. Now, my mother alone was in charge of his care.

"Hwain, what can I do alone?" She asked.

I tried to comfort her. I could feel that all the work of caring for Father was wearing her down. I worried about her health. "Mother, don't worry. I can help you. We can manage the situation together."

"God will help us." Mother replied.

We decided to share the responsibilities. I would help father exercise and my mother would bathe him. We became his complete medical team.

MOTHER, PHYSICAL THERAPIST

Dr. Ma, who was a department manager of New York Rehabilitation Medical Center, visited Father with his wife Dr. Cho. They came occasionally to check up on Father's condition, always surprised at how clean the patient was kept. They taught us several methods of exercise we could help my father to perform on our own. After examining him several times, they suggested we take Father to New York where he could stay at a hospital. His condition was very severe, and perhaps further treatment would do some good. The move seemed plausible if we could get Father to move his body at all, but it didn't seem likely. Still, we resolved to try.

Mother and I became his physical therapists. I massaged his legs from the center to the sides, pushing and rolling the flesh like dough. I would exercise his legs by folding and unfolding them at the knee, then pulling them down into a crossed position. I even wriggled his toes to increase blood flow. Then I lifted his arms up to the height of his shoulders and let them drop gently. His right arm did not yet move. My heart sank at the thought that he might never recover, but I never gave up hope. Father always smiled at me in appreciation.

Mother often peered out the window into the garden, where my father used to spend the day with his knees and hands in the dirt. Even though I visited each day to exercise my father, he and Mother were left alone in the aftermath of the day's often fruitless work. It was my mother who had to linger when hope lapsed; she had to survive the fight between life and death. The winter nights were long. It got dark at 4:30, and darkness brought on despair. Father would cry and shout through the long evenings. He'd moan strange, frightening sounds through the silent house, straining to move his arms and legs, which would tremble wildly, rattling the bed. Mother's heart beat hard and she broke out into cold sweats. Holding down his shaking arms, she'd shout, "God, please help me, please help me" over his own muffled outcry. After about an hour, father would become tired and his fits would peter away.

After giving him his sleeping pill, my mother would say, "Honey, I will pray for you. Don't cry, OK? If you cry, I can't pray. Close your eyes and stay calm, I will pray for you. God, with the help of the Holy Spirit, please cure your beloved son and let him stand up."

He would fall asleep just as she finished her prayer. Then mother slipped into bed aching all over.

THE SPEECH THERAPY

Although the speech therapist no longer came, mother had studied his methods assiduously and could put into practice everything she had seen him do. I usually helped my mother with the process, because it required his body to be lifted from the bed into a chair. As I raised him slowly with my arms wrapped around him, I would pray, "Oh, lord, please be with us. We will endure any other hardships. Please let father get well, please." Once seated, mother would rearrange his limbs and put large pillows under his arms so he would feel comfortable. He signaled to us whether he needed to be moved by crinkling his face or twitching his left arm.

Next, we'd have father exercise his lungs so that any abnormalities in breathing that might develop in the future could be prevented. The respiratory organ is very important, we learned, for speaking. After he performed the inhalation exercise more than 50 times, father would begin his speaking exercising by attempting to imitate vowel sounds.

I would model these: "a -, u-, o-." And he would attempt them in turn: "ma-, mu-, mo-."

The word we practiced most was "Um-ma," which means mother. This word was important, because he would need to use it to call mother whenever he needed anything. Father pushed his tongue to the front of his mouth, and we clapped our hands with pleasure. "We can see your tongue! Push a little more, a little more," we shouted.

AN ACUPUNCTURE AND THE PRAYER

The herb doctor finished performing his acupuncture on father around 6 pm that day. Knowing that Father had been lying in bed for the whole day, I lifted him so that he could sit up in a chair. It was already dinner time, but I assured my mother it was fine if I stayed late. My husband would be coming home late anyway. Father had been in pain all day; too much saliva had accumulated in his mouth, and it was difficult for him to swallow.

Father's left arm was the sole part of his body over which he seemed to retain some motor control. Today, moving it seemed to cause Father intense discomfort. He expressed that he couldn't move it in the same way as before. He could extend all five fingers, but only at the cost of extreme pain. When I saw the expression on my face, tears welled up in my eyes, and I hastily buried them into my father's shoulder as I repositioned his body, so mother wouldn't see. I'm sure he was trying to tell us something, but neither of us could make it out. It was probably better that we couldn't.

Mother told me that day that she had invited someone to come and pray for my father. He had placed his hands on my father's body. I knew that our Lord would heed our appeals if we asked with sincere belief, so I prayed that all our hopes be granted.

AT THE FATHER'S BEDSIDE

In the afternoons, I visited my father. Before even taking off my coat, I'd walk over to his bed to see him smiling up at me. He always welcomed me warmly that way. Opening his eyes wide, he'd flash them over to the blood pressure monitor. I'd measure it for him and tell him, "It's between 140 and 100. It's normal." Then he'd lean his head toward the black armchair at his bedside, which meant he wanted to be put in his chair. I'd pull his body up and place a pillow behind his back so that he would be sitting up. When his head didn't droop, I thanked God. Then I'd swivel his body and pull his legs down to the floor so he'd be seated on the edge of the bed. Then, we'd exercise his neck by moving it from side to side, the backwards and forwards.

The hardest part was moving his body the distance of three steps to the armchair. I would place his feet on the floor and his arms over my shoulders. My mother held his arms as I supported his upper body. His weight spread between the two of us was still hard to bear. The moment we got him into his chair, we'd huff out long exhalations of relief. Even Father would spit out a big sigh.

Then, Mother and I would eat dinner. Father always glanced over to the kitchen to indicate that he wanted me to keep Mother accompany while she ate. We often wondered when he would be able to join us.

Some days, we'd try to feed him. There was always the danger that he'd choke or be unable to swallow. "Don't swallow too fast," we'd warn him. "Just hold the food in your mouth until you're ready, then swallow slowly."

With every mouthful, I offered up a prayer to God. The little successes, each successful swallow gave us hope and reason for joy.

PREPARATION FOR THE NYU MEDICAL CENTER

My husband and I went to the office of Dr. Ma to discuss father's condition, so he could advise us as to the next step. His earlier suggestion that we send father to the hospital at NYU had given us hope. Mother and I had worked hard to get father's condition to improve, and now that it had, we felt we had the right to have hope for a recovery in the future. However, when we consulted with him for a second time, Mr. Ma's outlook was not as hopeful. In the car afterwards, my husband warned me not to expect too much. I didn't say a word.

After the meeting, we went straight to my mother's. I told her we had better apply for Medicaid immediately, and to do so we should empty the bank account. Before we left we put Father in his armchair and told him we'd be back in a little while. It was the first time in many weeks that my mother had been out of the house for very long. Just as we were turning the corner I asked my mother whether she had remembered to take her passbook. It turned out she'd forgotten it, and we had to turn back. When we arrived back at the house, we saw that father had an expression of extreme discomfort on his face. He had emptied his bowels in our absence. We were grateful that we'd turned back.

Mother had tears in her eyes when she closed her bank account to get father's medical aid. "Poor man," she said, swallowing them down.

X.

Blossom of the Golden Bell

THE GOLDEN BELL

EARLY IN THE MORNING I received a call from the registration office of the NYU medical center. They said that we needed to pay $87 more per day for the special room where my father would be staying. It would be available by next week; we just had to make a deposit.

On the way to school I stopped by my mother's house and sat at my father's bedside for a little while. Then I placed him in his wheelchair and we performed some of his daily exercises together, as my mother stood nearby watching. Atop a big wooden board made by his youngest son-in-law and which we placed on his lap, he practiced rolling a small cup by pushing it with his left hand. As the cup shifted across the board, I prayed, "Oh Lord, is it too much to ask that you cure father?"

Father soaked his feet for ten minutes in the hot water, then for two minutes in cold water. The doctors told us this would help smooth the circulation in his feet by stimulating the blood vessels.

As I changed the water in the plastic washbasin, I prayed again, "Lord, please help us. Please don't let our efforts be futile."

I prayed as I washed his right leg, and I prayed as I washed the other. I looked at myself reflected in the mirror behind Father's chair. I hid my tears from my mother as I held his feet in my hands.

Father turned his face to the window as he sat in his chair.

"Father, what do you mean?" we asked him. "Do you mean the car outside? Do you mean the door?"

Nothing we could guess was right, so we placed a pad beneath his left arm and asked him to write what was on his mind.

Very slowly, the word Gae appeared on the paper. "Ah————-! Gae Na Ri!" Mother and I agreed. Father had planted these golden blossoms in the garden last year, long before the stroke. They were now in full blossom, spreading up the walls like sunlight at dawn.

"Yes," we told him. "They're in bloom".

Three of us fell silent. I did not look out the window. I had seen the Gae Na Ri but had hardly noticed them, just as they seemed not to notice us and our suffering inside the walls of the house. It seemed to me then wonderful that they should be in bloom, that they shouldn't care, and that spring should come and pour out new beauty without hesitation, heedlessly, despite all.

THE DREAM

"Lord!
If my suffering is this much,
Then how much my mother's pain would be?
We are going to take Father
To NYU Medical Center tomorrow.
Knowing that this is the last method
That we can take, we are going to try once again.

Lord!
Please hear our prayers
Dedicated every morning and every night.

I believe that
You would not turn away from our sincerity.

Lord!
Mother believes that
Father who was standing in her grandson's dream
Is a revelation of you?

Lord!
What is the meaning of your showing,
In every family member's dreams.

Lord!
Today Se Hwan who is 2 years old
Said that he saw grandfather at outside.

Lord!
How nice it would be if it is real.

Lord!
It is 8 pm. Right now,
Mother would try to sleep
After giving father sleeping pill.

Lord!
Please have pity on us.

Lord!
Please be with us and give us a little hope
On the way to the hospital tomorrow.

Even though I knew it would be painful, I told my mother
we must prepare for my father's death. We had just to accept the
notion that death is an extension of life, and then it wouldn't seem
so unbearable, so unthinkable. But it was love that made it so difficult—the fact that we would have to be separated from someone

we loved so dearly. I've come to feel that it's not the life we mourn when we are faced with death, but love. A life without love is like death, so living is only worthwhile when there is love to enrich it, to make it more than mere existence.

THE NYU MEDICAL CENTER

NYU was a far friendlier place than I'd expected it to be. Every person involved in my father's care was a friend. There seemed such a chance of recovery there. Many of the other disabled patients were making progress, and this gave me and mother such comfort. The doctors and physical therapists seemed to us like angels performing miracles. Many of them were young and had devoted themselves to their work. They always seemed absolutely indomitable, going about their tasks with tireless enthusiasm—lifting the patients out of their chairs, helping them walk and move in new ways, and comforting them when they became frustrated. I spent the afternoons watching the physical therapists and was moved by their eagerness and patience. I had to stop myself from joining them in their efforts; I wanted to hold up the patients myself. Watching them and the people they served, I felt in my heart the preciousness of this life. I knew the patients would do anything just to be able to move a bit more, a bit wider, a bit farther, because that little bit meant so much. I saw in them the incredible human hunger for life. They only wanted every second to hold more possibility. They only wanted to be able. These people knew more about the limitations of being human than anyone, and yet the old lady with severed legs and the young man who was paralyzed from the waist down were both bursting with life. Even without motion, even in limitation, they were overflowing; the flame burnt on in them.

THE PRAYER

"Oh, lord,
I feel pain on my whole body and heart

I feel pain and pressure
On my head

On the dead end of narrow lane
That could not go forward or backward
I cry and call you loudly.

Oh, Lord,
Pity on us
And be with us

A day of 1 year
Summer is almost
On the door front
With Mother's endless care
Beside Father's bed
365 days have passed
Without any traces
But we are saying
We are not tired yet
We thank God
Father is still alive

Mother and I
Are not tired yet
With a hope. . .
With a small hope. . . ."

A DEADLY SITUATION

Mother discovered herself fallen asleep when she saw the clock
pointed 3 am. It had been 6 weeks since father had been moved
to the NYU Medical Center and commenced his physical therapy.
Though his progress was steady, Father continued to need constant
care and attention which his nurses and physicians often could not

give. The only person with whom he maintained a line of communication was my mother. My father did not have recourse to all the myriad words, gestures, movements, and faces that make up expression; all he had were his eyes, and the only person who could read their meaning was my mother.

Reading his requests, my mother busied herself with all the little tasks that maintaining her husband's comfort required. Before leaving each night, she'd make a final check in which she made sure that father's pillow was propped up comfortably beneath him, and check his arms and legs to see if they were in the right positions. When she was finished, she left the room without looking back. If she turned her head, she'd have to look into Father's eyes and see that he still wanted so much from her. If she looked back, she'd never be able to leave.

For the first few weeks I drove my mother to the hospital, but she preferred to hire a driver for the commute. She left home at 7:10 am and arrived at 8. The first thing she did was to rearrange Father's body, which always slumped out of position during the night. Each morning his face was flushed red and hot from the overnight fight. It was up to my mother to undo the ravages and usher in the new day and its new hopes; she washed his face in cool water and massaged his tightened features, then shaved his chin. Then the nurses came to take his blood pressure and temperature, and the physicians to begin the day's medical examination. Mother struggled to communicate with them always.

At 10:30 am, physical therapy began. Two male nurses lifted and placed father's body in a wheelchair. My mother would watch the transfer uneasily, wondering whether it hurt her husband, wishing the men could be more careful with him. During the first physical therapy session, the therapists exercised father's body by moving his arms and legs as he lied on a bed. Mother watched attentively, taking notes and learning the process so she could repeat it once they returned home.

Later in the afternoon was another session in which they tried to retrain father to eat by pushing pudding through his mouth. The doctors had to make sure each day that neither father's bronchus or the urethra was infected in the process. Mother treated father's urine during the day. At night, a tube was put into his urethra to allow the urine to flow automatically.

During the day, my father was secure in my mother's care. She was so helpful that the nurses and therapists paid special attention to him. But she could not stay to monitor the night time staffs, and Father had already suffered two fevers caused by infections.

One day, when I just got home from driving mother to the hospital, the phone rang. "Hwain, are you home already?" Her voice sounded unusually shaky.

"What happened, mother?"

"Father was bleeding. The nurses are treating him now, but you'd better come soon."

"I will be there right away, mother."

At the hospital the doctor informed me that the bleeding and infection had been caused by a folly catheters that had been improperly placed by a member of the night time staff. Father had been able to endure the many physical agonies that his condition and recuperation entailed, but this pain he could not endure. His face was white and he groaned out excruciating sounds that it hurt us to hear.

Father had lost too much blood, and the doctors found that his blood pressure had dropped dangerously. They decided to give him a blood transfusion. On his face they strapped an oxygen mask, and into his arm they pricked needles with wire attached to them, so the blood and drugs could flow through. A tube was inserted into his stomach and another into his urethra. We looked at him with pity as he lied there, sallow and motionless, blinks tears from his eyes slowly.

Watching my father in his suffering, I began to recognize in his out-lain body, still and withered as it was, the endurance of human life. Holes punctured his skin and tubes penetrated his flesh, performing the processes of metabolism where his body could not. Water and blood were supplied in turn. My father depended on constant medical attention. He needed help to survive. His life had been threatened and tested again and again, leaving his body irreparably damaged—and yet he lived.

After the commotion, the old routine resumed. My mother assumed her duties with new enthusiasm, and thanked God for her husband's survival. She now felt that there was some elemental strength and will in my father's soft and sallow body. He fought for his life just as she did. Human life wasn't as weak and susceptible as she had come to consider it. Rather, it was always fighting to uphold itself, always striving after its own continuation.

DISCHARGE FROM THE NYU

Father's condition did not improve even after two months in the hospital. The policy of the hospital was to discharge patients who showed no progress. The constant commute had also worn Mother out. Mother and I prepared for his discharge and learned various treatments we could give him at home. We knew that this was the last time we would receive aid from a hospital. Dr. Ma told us that it was a miracle father was surviving in his condition. It was Mother's utter devotion and Father's endurance that kept him with us, he said. We resolved never to give up on him.

We settled father back home. I could see my mother had taken the disappointment hard. When I came to visit late in the afternoon, after working through the day, Father no longer lit up with delight at the sight of me. Still, I spoke to him softly and exercised him. Then I realized that Father was trying to communicate something to me; he signaled to me to remove the tube from his arm. I had to stop myself from crying. "Father, now, be brave. We won't let you die. We cannot control the lives that God gave us, but we have to do our best."

I comforted my mother and told her that she should be prepared for any situation. The doctors had urged us not to expect too much, but mother still believed that her husband could recover. She knew that God could do anything, so why not this? I also held onto belief, waiting for God to answer our prayers.

A PEACE MAKER

Mother's daily routine drained her energy. Her health was weakening from the stress of caring for father. She could not confide her concerns in her children, so she entrusted them in God, begging him every night to give her the strength and skill to care for her husband without error or deficiency.

To help ease the workload, mother urged all of her children to be involved in their father's care. I lived nearby so I was more accessible than the others, who lived farther away and were all raising young children. Mother made up a schedule so that each child could come and help out when it was convenient. Each called their mother every day to ask about Father's condition and Mother's health. Mother always answered that she was fine, and that they need not worry.

By Confucian tradition, mother had right to demand the labor of her daughter-in-law, but she was not the kind of woman to exercise this right. She knew how busy Joon was finishing the last year of his fellowship, and that his wife had to care for her children. He visited every 2 to 3 weeks, and felt sorry that his wife had to stay home. Second daughter Hwa Bong visited Father even after she finished her night shift and bathed him. The youngest daughter Hwa Young drove over early every Sunday and stayed until the afternoon. Her husband worked outside, tending the lawn the way Father used to. He watered the grass and raked the leaves, and he also helped seat Father in his chair. Because of them, Mother could relax on Sundays.

To keep his mind active, mother constantly asked Father some questions. She asked him where the gardening tools were, or whether she ought to adjust the room temperature. When she misplaced things, she even asked whether he remembered where they were. She wanted to give him opportunities to think. She was constantly working to lift his spirits and to assure him that he still held an important place in our family, even in his incapacitation. We children worried that gathering for birthday parties or holiday celebrations would be too disheartening, having to celebrate in another room as Father lay alone. But mother's calm and assurance gave us the courage to meet and to be joyful. On Christmas, we exchanged presents at his bedside. At first, we were somber and our eyes filled with tears, but mother encouraged us out of our sorrow. She was the first to smile and laugh; the mood eased, and we followed in turn. We opened Father's gifts and presented them to him one by one.

"Honey, see how nice this quilt is? It'll keep you warm in the winter." Mother lifted the quilt to show father his granddaughter's gift. Father smiled and expressed his joy by turning his head both ways and drawing in a deep breath. All our families were grateful that we could worship beside him, and that we didn't have to feel guilty for enjoying ourselves.

Mother said, "I am so thankful that your father is still alive. I would be alone if it were not for your father." Her voice was bright and full of thanks. She comforted us with her ability to feel joy despite all that seemed so full of sadness to us. She brought peace to our troubled hearts.

"The praise of thanks
Is rising from my heart.

The thanks that
He has a consciousness
Even though he could not move
Give all of us a delight.
We all gathered here
Beside Father's bed.
We all family gathered around him.

We all laughed happily
Unpacking their presents.

We all forgot the sufferings of pain,
The difficulties of nursing.

The cheer of love,
And the cheer of thanks
Rise to the sky
Like smoke rises to the sky
Through a small chimney
Riding on dark air
In the midnight
That nobody could see.

Oh. . . .!
Our only wish
That is a life.
The passionate life
That we love to madness
Is the movement of life?

In this place
Where the thanks and love,
Sadness and agony crossed
A laughter is bursting out
And rises up to the sky
Without any words."

WITH HIS SON AND DAUGHTER-IN-LAW

After Father returned home, Mother continued to feel the strain of being his primary caretaker. But help came just in time. "Mother, do you mind if we come to live with you and Father? Our apartment lease is about to expire."

Mother was surprised at the suggestion of Joon's wife Sung. "How about your husband?"

"There is a room in his hospital where doctors could sleep. He can stay there and he could commute from here to the hospital." Sung assured her.

So it was settled, but my mother was skeptical as to whether the living arrangements would really suit everyone. She needed an extra set of hands to help maintain the house and care for Father, but she knew how difficult it was for a mother to live with her daughter-in-law. To ensure that the two families live harmoniously under one roof, and that her own difficulties inflicted no burden on her son and daughter-in-law, mother resolved to do most of the work herself. She was only grateful that she had this chance to live with her son and his new family. When Mother told Father about the new plans, he smiled.

Now six people were living in mother's house. Joon and his wife took the bedroom in the attic, and the two children each had a room on the second floor. Joon cleaned and renovated the barn to use as his study. The living room was split into two rooms so that mother's bedroom would be beside Father's, and the dining room was converted into the new living room.

Mother's house was filled with warmth and laughter once again. The children brought fresh sensations and joys to their grandparents, who watched them grow. Sung was a devoted helper, and Mother was pleased to have her good-natured daughter-in-law close by.

THE NEW HOUSE

Joon's fellowship was almost at an end. He had been in training at the North Shore Hospital for 6 years. Afterwards, he would be qualified as a medical specialist and could begin practicing. Joon began his search for a new place of employment in June of 1994. He considered his brother-in-law's hospital as a possible choice, and the family prayed over the decision. Mother worried about how she could manage Father's care alone if Joon and his family moved out.

Nevertheless, Mother began to prepare for the new situation and its challenges. Her son didn't say a word to her about his intentions, and this aggravated her concerns. Joon seemed unable to make a choice.

Following my suggestion, Joon began to look for a house to purchase through my real estate agent. Mother and I decided not to intervene in their decision, and to let them do what they thought was best for their family. But Sung Ja reported back to Mother everything about the houses they looked at, and asked her to accompany them on each round of visits. Mother was pleased that her son wanted to buy a house of his own and plant his family's life somewhere permanent. But she was also worried about her own welfare and that of her husband.

"Honey, if Joon buys a house and leaves, what do you think we should do? I think you want to go with them." Mother probed father's desires. Father answered that he would want to follow them. But either way, the choice wasn't theirs. They decided to entrust the matter to God.

Joon finally decided on a house, and when he did, he invited Mother and Father to live with his family there. Mother praised God for the generosity of her son and his wife: "Lord, thank you for giving me this beautiful opportunity. Please let us live together happily and peacefully. Help me to be a good mother to them."

THE VISIT OF FATHER'S SISTER

Mother had spent the last 3 years and 5 months caring for her husband. When he first had his stroke, the crisis distressed her so much she often felt she couldn't handle the responsibility or the effort it required not only to maintain his life, but also to sustain any hope or joy. She wished that father's brothers and sisters would come to help her, and perhaps to encourage her. But during the long stretch of father's incapacitation, she became father's and the entire family's stronghold. It was we who needed her.

News came that father's favorite sister whom he so desired to see would come to visit at last. Mother cautioned Father not to get to excited and so strain himself. "Honey, please don't cry. Your blood pressure will go up."

I left early in the morning to pick up my aunt at the hotel nearby. She and I waited outside Father's room while he was treated with acupuncture and Moxacautery. As the hours passed, my anxieties mounted. I worried their meeting would cause them both to suffer.

Finally, Mother called us into father's room. He uttered a loud cry in a voice we'd never heard before. My aunt began to cry and tried to soothe him. She wrapped her arms around him and said, "Don't cry, brother. Don't cry." They were just pulling out the acupuncture needles so my father's arms were tied to the bedside. Every time my aunt spoke, his eyes brimmed over with more tears. My mother's own tears had already dried up, and she seemed to stand tranquilly and assuredly above their sadness. "Honey, you promised you wouldn't do this," she said. "It's a good thing to see your sister." She showed him her bright smiling face that never faded. She kept her composure, and this gave him and his sister strength.

"Honey, isn't it wonderful to see your sister again?" Father shed his tears and lowered his voice and turned his head upwards towards the ceiling. He seemed to want to speak out, but his voice could not be heard.

FATHER'S BIRTHDAY

The 75th birthday of my father was June 13, 1995 and June 16 on the lunar calendar. My mother discussed the birthday party with her daughters-in-law and asked Reverend Kim to lead a family worship. The year before, we had invited all of our church members and relatives to our home to thank them for their concern over the health of my father, and to show them how well he was doing. One gathering like that was enough, my mother thought, so this time we decided that only our family members would come together for his birthday service.

Hwa Bong, the second daughter, was a registered nurse who worked the evening shift, so only her husband, Reverend Kim, was able to come. The youngest son-in-law worked until 8 pm in Manhattan, so he and the youngest daughter would come late. The eldest son-in-law, a medical doctor, had a meeting, so he too would arrive late for the service. The six people who had managed to gather as the service began were the first son Joon and his wife Sung and their son David, my father, my mother, and me.

Although there were only six people present for the service, Reverend Kim, as always, led it with as much composure and conviction as a man speaking to an assembly of a hundred. He would have preached the same way to an audience of one.

The sermon from Second Corinthians urged us to thank God for giving us the power to overcome human suffering and difficulty, to be grateful that our suffering enabled us to learn more about God and his love. God created between the brothers and sisters of our family a dialogue of love in which we could all share. We must all learn what faith was from our mother's belief, which was the foundation of our family's faith in Christ.

A portrait of Jesus Christ hung in the sharp angle below the room's high ceiling, and beneath this rested my father's bed, surrounded by birthday cards from grandchildren, sons, and daughters and a beautifully arranged basket of flowers sent by the youngest daughter. I felt what a holy place of worship this scene of love and devotion made.

The music of our hymns and the chorus of our prayers echoed upward to God.

As the worship ended, the door slammed shut behind the youngest daughter, arriving late with her husband. When my father saw his youngest son-in-law, tears fell from his eyes. Perhaps it was the joy of seeing them after a few weeks of separation that moved him to tears. Witnessing his emotion, Mr. Yoon, my mother, and all of us felt our own eyes moisten, but we quickly composed ourselves to greet our latecomers. "Christine, you've finally come! I am so glad to see you at this late hour. It's already 9 pm."

"Yes as it is." Christine and her husband Dae Hee replied. We welcomed them gladly. The first son-in-law arrived shortly after.

"All four of our brother and sisters have joined together. How wonderful it is."

We sat together around the dinner table, speaking earnestly to each other, full of pride and emotion for our reunion. Mother joined us and said, "Your father made a big concession. He allowed me to leave him and come here to be with all of you. I turned off the light. He's probably sleeping already after a day like this."

Mother sat among us and took part in our conversation. That night I woke before dawn and looked at the clock. It was only 5:00 am, and I'd gone to bed later than 1:00am the night before. For some reason I hadn't been able to sleep.

"She is such a mother," I thought. "I didn't force anyone to come, but everyone did. Mother made it so easy for us to come together."

Once again, I was surprised by an invisible power that the mother held. In the morning we children prepared several dishes and spoke to each other with love. I gave thanks for the implicit education my mother had given us. "Mother is surely such a woman."

I recollected conversation that I had with Yong Sun Hong a few days ago. "Sister, your mom is an extraordinary woman. She knows everything although she doesn't say anything. When I worked with your mother at YWCA, I watched her helping us. She was obedient to her husband without saying a word. Don't you think so? Sister, isn't that right?"

I just nodded my head without saying anything.

"Sister, that's not all. When I called your mother to say sorry because I never visited to help her with her husband, do you know what she told me? You are helping me by serving the YWCA. Sister, she is such a mother."

I remained silent and turned my face away. I looked out the windows to the greenness of the grassy, open lawn. I sighed, deep in thought.

"That's right. My mother is such a woman. She knows everything, even what is in our deepest hearts. There is no need to say anything."

I sat still for a few moments thinking of her, but the sound of the air conditioner woke me from my thoughts, and I came back to myself.

Epilogue

EVERLASTING BLESSING

DR. TAE WOO YOO, the founder of Korean Hand Acupuncture, visited my mother's house in a meeting arranged by Myung Hee Lee. She and I waited for Dr. Yoo at the Hilton Hotel in Fort Lee.

As soon as he arrived at the hotel from the airport, he was ready to visit my mother's house.

"Today is the 4th anniversary of my father's stroke. It attacked the left side of his body first, then the right side one week later. It's a miracle that he has been able stay alive all this time."

I explained to the doctor the progress of my father's medical condition over the last four years. Sitting in the backseat, he and Myung Hee Lee discussed my father's diagnosis.

"Father! Dr. Yoo came." My father suddenly burst out crying. He probably thought that this was his last chance to recover. Dr. Yoo checked my father's pulse and gave prescriptions to Myung Hee Lee. He laid out a few treatment options.

"His pulse and the overall condition of his heart are strong. He will improve because of the care his family has given him."

We couldn't detain him any longer, as his YWCA lecture would soon begin.

"Mother, we did everything we needed to do. Even Dr. Yoo came. . ."

After his visit, I spoke immediately to my mother as I always did. I hadn't had the chance lately, busy as I was with the many tasks given me. Even when I visited her there wasn't time to communicate alone because I would always busy myself caring for my father.

I spoke to her as we drove in my car, when our talk wouldn't interfere with my father's strict schedule of care. "I feel relieved now that Dr. Yoo has seen your father. In fact, Kim jipasnim and Koh jipsanim have been coming to look after him everyday."

"It seems there are no further complications. He just has to maintain his health through his heat treatments and acupuncture. There is no damage to his body even though he's been bedridden for four years."

Driving down Route 4 as the traffic slowed our progress home, I spoke to mother.

I reflected on her life up until this moment. She remained so full of joy and gratitude in every situation; she gave so much love to her children and grandchildren. She overcame so much difficulty, with a smile always ready at her lips and a heart always overflowing with love.

As I finish writing this book that I have devoted to my mother, I find that through her life suffering and strife were transformed into love. I have witnessed each day how God has blessed her, and how she has trusted him to do so. Through my mother and through my own life, I have come to believe that the suffering of life is a blessing from God. After ten years my father finally passed away. Now my mom still lives with me age of ninety eight, we are blessed!